Miss Coulton

My Eldest Brother

Vol. 1

Miss Coulton

My Eldest Brother
Vol. 1

ISBN/EAN: 9783337345334

Printed in Europe, USA, Canada, Australia, Japan

Cover: Foto ©Thomas Meinert / pixelio.de

More available books at **www.hansebooks.com**

MY ELDEST BROTHER.

A Tale.

By the Author of '*Our Farm of Four Acres;*' '*From Hay Time to Hopping.*'

IN TWO VOLUMES.

VOL. I.

London:
SAUNDERS, OTLEY, AND CO.,
66, Brook Street, Hanover Square, W.

1861.

LONDON:
F. Shoberl, Printer, 37, Dean Street, Soho.

MY ELDEST BROTHER.

CHAPTER I.

On my thirteenth birthday I commenced my battle with the stern realities of life. In the morning I arose a happy, thoughtless child; at night I was a woman in thought and action, burthened with heavy cares, and compelled, for the sake of others, to repress all expression of the deep sorrow with which my whole heart was filled.

It was, as I have said, my birthday, and when I met my family at breakfast I was greeted with many affectionate congratulations and good wishes.

As I took my seat at the table, I perceived three small packages by the side of my plate;

the first I opened contained a small beautifully-bound Bible, on the fly-leaf of which was written,

"To Nelly, on her thirteenth birthday, from her affectionate mother, Esther Travers."

I thanked my dear mother again and again for the welcome gift which marked her remembrance of the day.

"I am glad you are pleased with my present, Nelly dear," replied she kindly, "but now see what your other packets contain. Walter and Edmund are beginning to look impatient at your neglect of them."

Accordingly, I hastened to unclose a small parcel directed to me in a schoolboy's hand. It contained a gold locket, in which was prettily arranged hair of three different colours, which I immediately recognised as belonging to my mother, father, and sister. On the back was engraved "To Nelly; from her brothers, Walter and Edmund, on her birthday." While the box in which it was placed bore the saucy inscription of "To Miss in her teens."

I thanked my young brothers warmly for

this pretty and acceptable gift. I knew how long they must have appropriated their pocket money for the purpose of purchasing such an expensive article; and delighted as I was at receiving such a proof of their affection, I could not avoid expressing my regret that they should have expended so much on my account."

"Oh! don't trouble yourself about that, Nell," said Walter. "If we had not saved the money for the locket it would have been spent in trash, and now we shall always feel proud when we see you wear it, for it will remind us how manfully we resisted the appeals of 'Old Joe,' when he tried to seduce the money from our pockets by praises of the oranges and toffee he brought into the playground."

My third parcel held a present from my sister Esther. It was a pocket handkerchief, so beautifully and elaborately worked, and trimmed with lace of such exquisite fineness, that it might have served as a present to "Titania" herself.

On the envelope which enclosed it was

written, "To my darling Nelly; worked for her thirteenth birthday, by her loving and grateful sister, Esther."

My own dear Esther! This, then, was the work so hastily concealed, whenever during the last few weeks I had entered the room which for three years you had never quitted. Three years passed in the patient endurance of severe pain, unenlivened by even the faintest hope that you might one day rise from the couch on which you had spent such weary hours, and again know the blessings of health and the power of motion.

Loud were the expressions of admiration bestowed on this beautiful specimen of Esther's taste and industry; and my father, who all this time had been busily occupied in perusing the *Times*, disturbed by the voices of my brothers, laid aside his paper, and took the delicate piece of work from my mother's hand.

"So Esther did this," said he, when he had examined it for a minute or two. "My poor, poor Esther! It is another proof of her loving nature. While her fingers were busily employed with this work she forgot her own painful destiny, and thought only of the pleasure with which you would receive her gift."

My father sighed deeply as he laid down my present; and, rising from his seat, said to my mother—

"I shall be late at the bank to-day, I fear, if I wait for the boys to walk with me. They do not appear to have finished breakfast."

"Oh! yes we have, papa!" cried they together. "We shall be quite ready by the time you are."

"But what is the matter, Nelly?" said Walter, turning to me; "you look as if you were going to cry."

And indeed it was with difficulty I refrained from doing so. Cormorant that I was for affection, I was wounded beyond the power of concealing my emotion that no memento of my birthday had been offered by my father. He was on the point of quitting the room, when my brother's exclamation drew his attention to my woe-begone face.

"Cry!" said he. "No; Nelly would never do so unlucky a thing on her birthday. She would be too much afraid of Martha's scolding, even if she had cause for weeping."

"Dear George," said my mother, "do not tease her—you know how sensitive she is; and I am sure it is the pain of thinking you had forgotten what day it is, which causes her to look so wretched."

"Is that it indeed, Nelly?" said my father, as he put his hand into the pocket of his morning-gown, and drew a small morocco case from it. "Never form opinions too hastily, my child. Let this show you that papa did not forget his little daughter on the important day she entered her teens."

He opened the case and placed it in my hand. A beautiful little gold watch laid within it.

What girl of thirteen would not have received such a present with delight? I had often wished for such a treasure, but without the hope of possessing it. Yet now, when it was unexpectedly mine, I placed it on the table almost without a glance, and burst into a violent passion of tears.

"Good heavens! Nelly," said my father, impatiently, "what can be the matter with you? I have purchased for you the article, of all others, I knew you coveted, and you receive it as if I had presented you with some fatal omen."

I could not speak for some seconds, and my dear mother again interposed in my behalf. She seemed to know by intuition the feelings of her children; and read my heart as correctly as if it had been a book open to her inspection.

"Nelly is sorry that papa's gift is so costly. Had you placed it with the others she would have been delighted with it, both for its beauty and as a mark of your affection. Now that she has suffered you to see her disappointment when she imagined you had forgotten her, she fears you will attribute it to a selfish feeling, and, therefore, the value of your gift makes her unhappy. Is not that what you feel, Nelly?"

"Oh! yes, mamma, I would rather papa

did not give me the watch. Indeed, indeed, it was not for the value of the present I wished to receive one. It was the thought only that I cared for."

"Nelly dear," said my father, as he drew me towards him, "you must correct this fault in your character; such morbid craving for tokens of affection is not healthy. It will in time make you selfish and exacting, and, by centreing your thoughts too much on yourself, induce a false sentimentality of character, which will eventually bring on the evil you so much dread, and estrange from you the regards of those from whom you are most anxious to receive affection."

He kissed me tenderly, as he once more prepared to leave the room; and I could not answer his kind rebuke of my selfishness for the deep sobbing which seemed as if it would burst my heart.

"Now, Nelly," said my youngest brother Edmund, "I think it is very unkind of you to behave as you are doing. You know Martha says there is nothing so unlucky as to cry on a birthday. One would think you wanted to bring misfortune into the house."

Here Walter interrupted with "And we are to be so very jolly to-day. Don't you remember, papa, that you promised to take us to the theatre on Nelly's birthday; so you must come home early for the purpose."

My father kindly promised he would return before his usual hour, and shortly after left the house with the two boys, for the purpose of walking to the City.

Shortly after their departure, I went up stairs to my sister's room, which I was never allowed to enter till dressed in a white wrapper; she was lifted from her bed and placed on the couch, on which she reclined during the greater portion of the day.

How beautiful she looked, as she lovingly embraced me, and wished me many, many happy returns of that day! Pain and long confinement to a sick room had robbed her cheek of every trace of the lovely colour which once bloomed on it, but no shade of the sallow hue, usually seen on the face of an habitual invalid, had usurped its place. Pale and pure as a lily was the face of my sweet sister, in which every delicate blue vein could be distinctly traced.

I never saw eyes that in the least resembled Esther's: they were of the dark but vivid blue of the sky on a bright starlight night. So soft, and yet so lustrous in their beauty. They were such loving eyes, too, and always looked as if they were entreating for affection in return for that she so lavishly bestowed on all around her.

Though unable to move on the couch without assistance, Esther was never idle; supported by pillows, she worked several hours daily, and was never so happy as when she could surprise her friends by presenting them with some article she had secretly worked for them.

No one was in her confidence but Martha on such occasions, and very proud she was of her young lady's beautiful work. This faithful servant was in the room when I entered it, and had her birthday gift ready to offer me. It consisted of a cookery book, handsomely bound, and my name and the date on which it was presented to me by "Martha Taylor," printed in gold letters inside the cover.

I thanked her warmly, and assured her with perfect truth that I was delighted with her present.

"Oh, Miss Nelly, I thought you would like it," said she. "It is quite time now that you begun to make yourself useful. Suppose I was to die, who would make the nice jellies and broths that your mamma and Miss Esther almost live on? And I was thinking that if you liked to come into the kitchen this morning, I would show you how to make the cabinet pudding your papa is so fond of."

Martha had lived with my mother from the time of her marriage. She had nursed all her children. And when three years previously Esther had fallen down stairs, and permanently injured her spine, Martha had the sole charge of the invalid night and day, and had since been jealous of any one else superseding her in the duty of attending on her.

But Martha had many other occupations. Not the least important of which was superintending the cooking; and, therefore, she was compelled to give up her charge to my mother for some hours in the middle of the day.

For many months after my sister's accident gloom and sorrow hung over our home. The injuries she had received caused such agony that occasionally her screams filled every heart with terror and anguish. These frightful attacks of pain subsided after a time, and my father and mother ventured to indulge the hope that their child might be restored to health. But, alas! their fond anticipations were soon dashed away. Esther might live, but it must be only as a helpless, crippled invalid!

It was a day of bitter grief when this dreadful intelligence was communicated to them by the skilful surgeons who attended the poor girl.

Esther herself received it with resignation. "I knew it must be so," she said to Martha. "I felt that I should never again rise up and take my place among them all; but how much have I to be thankful for, in being told that I shall not again be liable to the dreadful agony I formerly suffered. And then I know how I shall be loved and petted by you all. After a time I shall become reconciled to my fate, and we shall be happy and contented as before."

"Happy and contented as before!" Who that heard Esther utter these words would have imagined that a dark curtain in our home concealed a skeleton which had filled our young hearts with fear and apprehension for the last six years?

True, the curtain was only occasionally lifted; and each time it was raised we hoped it would be for the last time. Months had passed since last it had cast a shadow over the tranquillity of our home, and on this morning of my birthday not a foreboding of evil from its presence dimmed the gaiety of our hearts.

It was with a light step and happy heart that I followed Martha into the kitchen, to receive my first lesson in the noble science of cookery. Provided with a large white apron, and with my sleeves pinned back, I obeyed the directions of my *chef* in preparing the famous pudding. I carefully weighed spices and measured out wine, while Martha herself beat up the eggs—a task she considered too laborious for me; and when all the good things, which were to produce so great a whole, were properly mixed and compounded together, I left the kitchen and hastened to my sister's room, to astonish my mother and herself with my wonderful facility in acquiring culinary knowledge.

Four o'clock arrived at last—the hour at which my father had promised to return to dinner. My brothers had long been home, and, like myself, were waiting impatiently for his appearance. I was dressed ready for the evening, and wore my locket round my neck, fastened to a small gold chain my mother had lent me for the purpose. Very seldom did my mother leave home; never in the evening; and she had promised to read some interesting new work to Esther during our absence.

Walter and Edmund were looking from the window, hoping to see their father approach.

Suddenly, Walter exclaimed, "Here's a cab coming, Nelly—I think it must be papa!" And almost before I could reach the window the vehicle stopped at our door.

"It is papa!" cried my brothers, and rushed from the room to open the door. I followed, and as I entered the hall saw a stranger descend from the carriage.

"It is not papa, Walter. Come back directly," cried I.

"It is, Nell!" replied he, in a tone of horror. "Look! there are two strangers with him, and they are helping him out of the cab. Look! he cannot walk."

Oh! miserable, miserable truth. It was indeed my father, who, supported by the strangers, was being borne into the house, to all appearance incapable of motion.

They looked inquiringly at me as they entered. I knew they wanted to be told where they were to place their helpless burthen, and I opened the door of the drawing-room and signed to them to enter. I could not speak—I moved like one in a dream—but I thought I must not let my mother know of this, or it will kill her.

"The gentleman has been seized with a fit in the street," said one of the strangers; "he was taken to the nearest surgeon's, and he advised his being brought home at once. We discovered his address by some letters in his pocket. You had better send directly for a medical man."

Walter, who with a face pale with horror had followed me into the room, said, " I will run for Mr. Spencer," and instantly left the house.

During the few minutes he was absent, I could only stand gazing in speechless agony on the beloved parent who laid senseless on the floor of the room.

When Mr. Spencer arrived he looked greatly shocked at the sight he beheld, and hurriedly asked a few questions of those who had brought my father home, relative to his sudden seizure. They repeated the tale already told to myself.

"My poor child," said the kind surgeon, turning to me, "do you think you can keep your mother out of the way while we take your father up stairs. If she is suddenly apprised of this sad thing I fear the shock might prove fatal to her."

At these words I seemed at once restored to strength and composure: they were the echo of my own thoughts. I knew it would kill my mother should she see my father in that state, without preparation for the anguish which awaited her.

Martha was now in the room, loosing his neckerchief and chafing his death-cold hands, while the tears rolled down her cheeks. "Go, Miss Nelly, to your sister's room, and contrive some way to detain my mistress there. I will do all that can be done for your father, you may safely leave him to me. But don't —pray don't—let your mother or Miss Esther know of this; it will be the death of both; keep it from them for a time at least."

I turned to leave the room, but before I quitted it, said to Mr. Spencer, "Will he live?"

"I cannot say," was the answer; "all that human skill can do for him shall be tried. It is an attack of paralysis, and I greatly fear the result. But go to your mother. I will send at once for Dr. H——, and when he has given his opinion then she must know of this terrible calamity. Keep her in ignorance of it till then if possible."

I kissed my father's forehead, and left the room. My brothers were waiting for me outside the door, weeping bitterly.

"Oh! Nelly, Nelly, will papa die?" sobbed Walter.

"God knows, dear. Pray to Him to help us in this dark hour. Go to your room and keep quiet till I come to you."

The poor children obeyed me directly; and I, with a smile on my face and a heart aching with misery, entered Esther's room.

"I have been wanting you some minutes, Nelly," said my mother, holding up the work on which she had been engaged. "Come and let me see whether this will look pretty in your hair. Kneel down and I will fasten it on."

I did as she requested. "No, Nelly," said she, after she had altered the arrangement of the ribbons two or three times, "it won't do; you look better without it; and so I am sure papa will think. But is it not time he was home, dear? You will be late in arriving at the theatre if he is not here shortly."

"The very apprehension of such a terrible catastrophe has made Nelly look pale," said Esther. "But cheer up, dear, papa will eat his dinner all the more quickly for being behind his time. I know he will not suffer you to lose a single word of either of the three pieces you are to be delighted with to-night."

I have suffered much mental agony, I have gone through many dreadful scenes since that day, but anything like the misery I then endured I never experienced after.

I sat quietly in the room. I heard the light jesting of my sister, and answered with composure the questions of my mother, and nothing of the agony I felt was visible in voice or look. One thought was always in my mind, "I shall have to tell them that my father is dead, and then they, too, will die."

Presently Martha came to the door. "Miss Nelly, will you come and see to your pudding?"

"Oh! that is the cause of your silence, is it, Nelly?" said my sister. "Your thoughts are in the saucepan with your pudding. You are fearful it will not turn out well, and that you will be disgraced for ever in the eyes of Martha by your failure."

I walked leisurely to the door, and closed it softly behind me. Martha was waiting on the landing.

"You must go and speak to Mr. Spencer," she whispered; "he says he must go for a short time, but wishes to see you before he leaves."

I followed her to the room into which my father had been carried. He was placed in bed, and was as insensible as when I had left him. I needed not to ask Mr. Spencer a single question. I knew that no change had taken place during my absence.

"I must leave you," said he, "and go myself in search of Dr. H——; every moment is of value; and I will return with him as quickly as possible. In the interim nothing can be done. I sent for you to give you this paper; it was tightly grasped in your father's hand, and I had considerable difficulty in removing it. The persons who brought him home informed me he was reading it at the moment he fell."

I took the letter—for such it appeared to be—and was about to place it on the table, but as my eye glanced at it, I observed, with a shudder, that the writing was well known to me.

Yes; the family skeleton was again uncovered, and the sight of it had killed my father!

CHAPTER II.

I LEFT my father's room with the paper in my hand, and as soon as I reached my own, prepared to read it.

It was from my wretched brother, from my mother's eldest born; who, from the time he was twelve years old to the present hour, when he was two-and-twenty, had been the plague-sore of our home. Liar and thief from his early boyhood, every means had been tried for his reformation but without effect.

Wherever he had been placed he had disgraced himself and dishonoured his father's name; for weeks at a time he would disappear from his family, and leave no trace of his whereabouts; then, when my father had used every means to discover his lurking-place in vain, he would suddenly write from some haunt of infamy, and say that he was ill, dying, surrounded by wretches who had robbed him of all that he possessed, even to the clothes in which he had entered their den of vice.

Then would my poor father go to the place from whence the letter of the wretched boy was dated, and rescue him from the miseries he was enduring.

Nursed back into health and strength, clothed, and, as his parents fondly ventured to hope, in his right mind, he was once more treated as a son, no mention ever made of his past transgressions, and he was allowed to take his place again in the family circle.

For a time he would behave respectfully to my father, be affectionately attached to his mother and young brothers and sisters; and then, when confidence was placed in him, he would abuse it as before, and once again did the sight of my father's indignation, and my mother's tears, fill our young hearts with sorrow, and cause us to think with anger and dread of him who so frequently darkened the sunshine of our home by his base and miserable selfishness.

At last the climax of his misconduct appeared passed. He had absented himself for a longer time than usual; when one night a loud knocking at the street door roused every one from sleep. It was a policeman; who answered my father, when he inquired the reason of the disturbance: a man, apparently dying, extended on the door steps, had feebly entreated him to procure him admittance into the house—his home, as he stated.

No doubt crossed my father's mind as to the identity of the wretched object who was carried into his house in the dead of night.

Taken at once to his own room—always kept in readiness for him—and a surgeon sent for, it was discovered that he had received two severe wounds in his side, which had, apparently, recently been inflicted with a common table knife.

How he came to his home in that state and at that hour was never known. For weeks he laid hovering on the very verge of death; and when at length his intellect was clear enough to understand the questions put to him on these points, his only answer was a shudder of horror and a passionate entreaty that his last absence from home might never be mentioned, or the manner in which he returned to it.

The lesson had been terrible, but it appeared effective.

For nearly two years he remained with us quiet, humble, and penitent. The remembrance of his errors appeared blotted from the memory of all, and he was once more trusted and beloved.

Still something must be done for his future welfare—some employment be found for him.

A friend of my father's—a merchant in Liverpool—offered to receive him into his counting-house, providing that my father and some other responsible person would become sureties for his integrity in rather a considerable sum of money.

I remember the grave conversations which took place between my parents on this point, and that my father said "I will myself take all the responsibility, and trust to Henry's promises of future good conduct; but I will not suffer a friend to run the risk of being injured by the misconduct of a son of mine."

That, however, would not satisfy Mr. Rivers—he must "have his bond"!

Let my father provide the proper securities, and there was the place for his son. And it was one which, if he conducted himself properly, would eventually lead to wealth and honour.

My mother earnestly advised my father to accept the offer made him by his oldest and dearest friend, and allow him to join in giving Mr. Rivers the required security.

Mr. Lancaster well knew that Henry had been wild and imprudent, though he was ignorant of the full extent of his misconduct, and from friendship for my father was willing to risk something for the welfare of his erring son.

"Accept this generous offer, George," said my mother. "I know Henry's character better than you do; he has been, as you say, a thief, but he is likewise a coward, and will not rob where detection will be followed by punishment. He has hitherto confined his depredations to his own family, and should he—which God in his mercy forbid—again fall back into crime, it is his own family on whom it will be committed."

Persuaded against his own conviction to allow his friend to join him in giving Mr. Rivers the security, my father accompanied his son to Liverpool, and returned thankful for the safe refuge he had found for him.

The duties Henry had to discharge were not laborious; they did not require more hours at the desk than was consistent with the preservation of his health, and for a handsome sum, to be paid yearly by my father, he was to reside in the family of Mr. Children, the head clerk of Mr. Rivers.

We heard frequently from Henry for several months after his departure from home. He said he was happy, that his duties were light and pleasant, and that he was treated by Mr. and Mrs. Children as kindly as if he were their own son.

"Don't fear, dearest mother," wrote he, "that I shall ever again disgrace you, and pollute my own soul by falling back into the slough of infamy into which I formerly allowed myself to sink. Thank God! my eyes have been opened to the depths of my iniquities, and His own merciful forbearance towards me; like the forgiving father in the parable, you may say, 'This my son was dead, and is alive again, was lost and is found."'

Mr. Rivers, too, rejoiced our hearts by occasionally writing to my father in praise of his son's steady attention to business and general correct conduct.

This pleasant state of things had continued for nearly twelve months, and though latterly we had not so frequently heard from Henry, no apprehension of evil saddened the hearts of any of his family. On the morning of this fatal day, my father had said, just as he was leaving the house, "I dare say I shall find a letter from Henry at the Bank;" and so he had—the letter I now held in my hand.

I have heard that to drowning men the whole of their past existence is shown to them in a moment of time; so it was with me as regarded the misdeeds of my brother;

every evil he had committed, every misery he had inflicted, arose vividly before my mental vision—and though I had not read a line of the letter, which had been taken from my father's grasp, I knew that it contained evidence of fresh crimes perpetrated by the son so tenderly beloved, so frequently forgiven.

"Help me once more, my father! I have again been assailed by temptation, and again fallen, and I shall stand as a felon at the bar of justice if you do not extricate me at once from the perils which surround me. I have spent money on myself which was entrusted to me in the way of business, and in the hope of replacing it, I have passed nights at the gambling-table, and each night left it more deeply involved in difficulties. Last week I had to render an account of the various sums I had received. To avoid present detection, I obtained money on a bill—sufficient to cover my deficiencies—to that bill I forged the name of Mr. Rivers. On Saturday—three days only from the one on which I am writing

—this must be discovered. Send me, immediately, three hundred pounds, or your wretched son is lost for ever.

"H. T.

"P. S.—I need not remind you that in the event of my defalcations becoming known, not only yourself, but Mr. Lancaster, will suffer heavy loss. So if not for my sake, for your own and his, send the money I require directly."

Was it to be wondered at, that the strong man fell, stricken to the earth while reading this letter from his base and miserable son?

I knew and felt that, much as the letter itself must have shocked the poor father, it was the inconceivable baseness of the postscript which had driven the shaft into his heart. That placed in the perilous condition of a forger, liable each moment to detection, he could calmly endeavour to extort money from his father by threats of the injury he could inflict on the friend who had so nobly pledged himself for his honour, must, I felt, have filled the cup of anguish offered by his degraded child.

The bitter grief for my father's illness seemed lost in the indignation which filled my heart against my brother.

I felt that my father must die, that my mother, Esther, and my young brothers would have no friend or adviser but myself, and for their sakes I resolved to harden my heart against the miseries I foresaw.

Should my father's murderer dare to intrude into the home he had desecrated, I myself would denounce him to the employers he had wronged. All these sad and bitter feelings passed, as I have said, through my mind in a short time.

When I had read the letter twice through, every word it contained seemed burnt into my memory. I shall never want it more, I thought, and was about to destroy it, when I suddenly remembered I ought to show it Mr. Lancester, as it deeply concerned his interests, so I placed it in my bosom for present security, and then returned to my father's room.

He had never moved from the moment he

was placed on the bed, and it was difficult for Martha to induce me to believe he still breathed.

"Oh! Miss Nelly," said that faithful friend, "what will become of your mother and Miss Esther, if this great evil falls upon them?"

"I will take care of them," said I, in a quiet, composed voice.

"You, poor child! What can you do?"

"All that can be done, dear Martha. I feel that God has given me a heavy charge, and I will pray for strength to bear it. Dry your tears, dear friend, we have to think of others, not of ourselves. We must bury our grief in our own hearts, while we strive to pour consolation and hope into those of others."

At this moment, a low knock at the street door was followed quickly by footsteps on the stairs, and Mr. Spencer and Dr. H—— entered the room.

"You must leave us, poor child," said the former, as soon as he had asked if any alteration had taken place in the patient, and he quietly led me to the door.

"Let me remain," said I, imploringly. "I may be of some use—and I will neither speak nor move, unless you require me to do so."

"No!" said he, firmly; "I will see you down-stairs, but now you must go."

It was a long time before they entered the room where, with a throbbing heart, I was waiting to hear the sentence of life or death passed on my beloved father.

"My dear little girl," said Dr. H——, kindly, "have you no friend who will come to you in this sad emergency? You are too young to have the care and responsibility of the whole family on your head—and Mr. Spencer has explained to me the precarious state of health both of your mother and sister."

"No!" replied I; "we have no friend whom my mother would like to have with us at such a time as this. But tell me of my father! Oh! sir, can you save him to us?" He looked at me compassionately, but did not speak. "Let me know the truth," cried I; "it will be best for me—it will be better for us all—that I should know it."

"You may trust her," said Mr. Spencer. "She has great power of endurance when suffering bodily pain, and I think she will not prove deficient in courage when called on to bear the still more terrible agony of such a trial as this."

Tenderly did then the kind physician communicate to me the dreadful intelligence, that he had no hopes of my father's recovery, that the shock had been so severe he feared he could never rally from the state of insensibility in which he still laid. Still, certain remedies were to be tried, and it was possible they might prove effective.

"Martha appears perfectly competent to the task of nursing your father," said Mr. Spencer, "but you will require another person to aid her; she will not be able to remain in the room during the night. I will send a nurse from the hospital."

I earnestly entreated him not to do so. I knew my mother's horror of hired nurses, and that she would not be prevented from herself attending to my father when acquainted with the state in which he was.

The time had arrived when it must be communicated to her.

I would not accept the offer which Mr. Spencer made, of himself acquainting her with the calamity which had befallen her. I was to be the consoler of her sorrow, her helper in this great trouble, and no one but myself must witness the agony with which the knowledge of it would be received.

"It shall be as you wish, then," said Mr. Spencer; "but I will remain till you have executed your painful duty. I fear the shock may prove injurious to your mother, and should you require my assistance, I will hasten to you at once."

No apprehension had crossed my mind that my mother might suddenly appear amongst us. Esther was never left alone even for five minutes, and till Martha or myself relieved her, I was certain she would remain patiently with my sister.

As I entered the room this time, my face must have betrayed that I had evil tidings to impart. My mother looked up as I opened the door, and with a quiet gesture of her hand prevented my advancing towards her.

"I will come this instant, Nelly," said she. "Esther, darling, Martha shall be with you immediately."

She followed me directly from the room, and as she opened the door, whispered, "Don't let Esther know of it—something terrible has occurred, I know—come into my room, and let me hear what it is."

I was astonished at the calmness with which she spoke, and ventured to hope she might bear the tidings with more fortitude than I had dared anticipate. I followed her to her room in silence. The moment I had closed the door, she said,

"Now, Nelly, tell me your errand. I can guess it is some evil connected with my son." My mother was always excessively pale. It was not possible for any illness or emotion to render her more colourless than she habitually was, but now the pure white of her complexion was changed to ashey gray, as in a hoarse whisper she said, "tell me the truth at once—is he dead?"

I was so alarmed at her awful appearance, and the stern composure with which she waited for my answer, that it was almost a relief to me to reply, "No, mother! Dearest mother! Henry is not dead—I do not know that he is ill."

Not a suspicion of the truth crossed the mind of my poor mother. Trouble and misfortune were associated in her mind with Henry alone, and of him only did she now think.

"It is my father, mother—my dear, dear father!"—and as I proceeded, all my boasted fortitude forsook me, and I, who had imagined I possessed the power of wholly controlling my own feelings, and that I could soothe the anguish of others, burst into an agony of sorrow at the very moment of all others when I ought to have preserved my composure.

I do not know—I never can remember—how at last my mother comprehended the full extent of her misery. I know that for some time she lay extended on the floor of the room, and that I rushed frantically for Mr. Spencer.

When restored to consciousness, no persuasions could induce her to remain out of my father's room.

"I shall have strength given me to perform my duty, do not fear," said she, in answer to Mr. Spencer's remonstrances. "While my husband lives, I do not quit him. Go, Nelly, to you I commit the charge of Esther and your brothers. Try, my child, to subdue your emotion, that you may support and comfort them under this heavy affliction."

CHAPTER III.

I PERFORMED the duties my mother had committed to me—I attended to my helpless sister, and to the comfort of my young brothers—and then, when they went to rest, I sat quiet for some time, while I endeavoured to reflect on the steps I ought to take relative to the letter of my unhappy brother. I had no right to keep Mr. Lancester in ignorance of his guilt.

The immediate payment of the sum he had demanded might prevent that gentleman from incurring a heavy loss.

How ought I to act? Should I enclose the fatal letter to him, and leave to his own discretion what steps he considered best to take. No! I could not suffer that evidence of

Henry's unworthiness to pass out of my hands. I would send to Mr. Lancester, and entreat him to come to me at once.

Impatiently did I wait the return of my messenger. Mr. Lancester's house was not very far distant from our own, and almost before I expected a reply I was told he was in the drawing-room.

He was greatly shocked when informed of my father's illness—how bitter was the task of telling him it was occasioned by his son's profligacy. I gave him the letter, and told him how it was removed from the insensible hand of my father.

Dreadfully was this kind friend grieved with its contents. I don't think one thought of his own possible heavy loss crossed his mind. It was wholly filled with commiseration for our unhappy fate.

"Does your mother know of this letter?" inquired he.

"No; she is ignorant of the event which has given the death-blow to my father."

"Then never let her become acquainted with it. I will start for Liverpool, and see this unworthy son of an honourable father. I will write and tell you all I can learn respecting him, if I do not return myself as soon as a letter would reach you. God bless and preserve you, Nelly! trust implicity to His love and mercy for strength to sustain you in this bitter trial."

Somewhat relieved by the discharge of this painful duty, and by the kindness of Mr. Lancester, I returned to my father's room. There all remained the same. My mother sat motionless as a statue by the side of the bed. But, oh! the expression of hopeless misery with which she regarded me as I crept to her side.

Through the long, long hours of night, did we together watch by the beloved father and husband, who, unconscious of our presence, lay still as death before us. All the more wretched was that night's watching from the absence of all the usual occupation of a sick room. We could do nothing but sit and look on the beloved face—there were no medicines to be administered, no nourishments to be prepared.

Who that has passed a night by the sick-bed of one dearly beloved, does not remember the keen agony with which the first dawn of day is beheld—that cold, gray light, which gradually extinguishing the one burnt in the chamber, seems to throw additional gloom over every object it reveals—the expiring lamp, the neglected grate, the table strewn with the various articles required during the weary and painful watch, the pale faces and shivering forms of the watchers, and the peculiarly ghastly hue it imparts to the face of the sick person—all appear to stamp the reality of misery more distinctly on the heart—and as the sun mounts higher and higher, till its beams pierce through the curtained windows of the room, it is with feelings of bitter sadness we endeavour to exclude its admission, as if it shone in mockery of our own wretchedness.

The day wore on, and brought no mitigation of our misery. Esther had insisted on being told all the circumstances concerning her father's illness, and bore the knowledge better than I could have expected. I had dreaded to impart the sad truth to her, for I feared the emotion it would occasion might bring on a return of the frightful spasmodic cramps from which she formerly suffered.

But I did not know her brave heart; she had been so long out of our working-day world, so carefully guarded from any of the petty troubles of our daily life, that I was surprised to find a woman's thoughts and feelings had imperceptibly replaced those of a child.

She was three years older than myself, but ever since her accident I had appeared to take the elder sister's place. She was considered apart from the rest—one to be loved and prized by all, but not to participate in the troubles and anxieties which might cross our paths.

I would have kept from her, if possible, the knowledge of Henry's misconduct, but she would know all, and I was compelled to show her the letter which had given the death-blow to my father. I told her what I had done respecting it, and of the kindness which Mr. Lancester had shown towards us.

"Dear Nelly," said she, when my tale was ended, "you have done all things rightly; but you must not forget that I am older than yourself, and though I am a helpless cripple, giving much trouble where I would thankfully give aid, yet I can reason and act in some things, perhaps, more wisely than yourself. Let me see Mr. Lancester when he returns, and let us together hear the results of his interview with Henry. But surely, Nelly," added she, "my mother has asked for him ere this?"

"Thank God, Esther, she has not mentioned his name! How dreadful it would be to tell her he is the origin of all our sorrow!"

"And in order that she may have no suspicion of it, he must be sent for at once, if, indeed, he does not return with Mr. Lancester."

I looked at my sister in astonishment; no thought of Henry again residing in the home into which he had brought such desolation ever crossed my thoughts, and it was in a tone of indignation I replied, "Esther, would you see our mother receive with affection the murderer of our father?"

"Dear Nelly, yes. I would give her all the consolation she is capable of receiving. Let the knowledge of Henry's crime be confined to our own bosoms; Mr. Lancester will not betray it, and the dreadful consequences it has produced may perhaps be the means of bringing him to repentance."

I with difficulty repressed the bitter words which arose to my lips as I listened to my sister. I believed that what Henry had always been he would continue to the end. I limited the power of God's mercy, and did not remember that those who were called at the eleventh hour received the same payment as those who had laboured from the first.

Late in the evening Mr. Lancester returned. He had seen my brother, and told him of the effects produced by his cruel letter. At first he was incredulous, and believed that Mr. Lancester wished to frighten him.

With difficulty was he convinced of the truth; and when he was, his remorse was described by our kind friend as something fearful to witness.

He rolled on the ground in convulsive agony, and declared he could never more look in the face of his mother.

After a while this tempest of reproach abated, and then it appeared, from his communications to our friend, that he was not even placed in the fearful predicament he had represented in his letter.

He had not committed forgery; he had spent some money entrusted to him, but not to a quarter of the amount he had represented, although, to extort that sum from his father's fears, he had written that wicked letter.

More fiercely than ever did my anger burn against him. "I ought to have known it!" I exclaimed, when Mr. Lancester had ended his narrative. I ought to have remembered the words I once heard my mother use:

"He is too much a coward to rob any but his own family!"

"Why, Ellen," said Mr. Lancester, in a surprised tone, "are you sorry your brother has not committed a felony?"

"Not committed a felony?" replied I, passionately. "Is not murder a crime? And has he not been guilty of that?"

"Nelly, you must control your vehemence, for the sake of others," said Esther. "Henry's conduct admits of no palliation; but we are his sisters, and must be thankful he is not so guilty as we feared."

"Where is he?" inquired she of Mr. Lancester.

"At my house."

"Dear, kind, generous friend, how shall we ever repay you for such kindness?"

"My poor children," was his answer, "I have known and loved your father from the time we were boys, like Walter and Edmund. I will act by his children as I know he would have done by mine, had they been placed in similar circumstances. I think the violence of Henry's grief may prove injurious to your mother, and till she wishes to see him he had better remain with me."

CHAPTER IV.

I CANNOT record the events which marked, day by day, my father's progress towards the grave. He never unclosed his eyes during the six nights and days we watched in hopeless misery beside him. All this time my mother never left him.

But when the semblance of death was changed for the reality, she kissed the dead face she had loved so fondly, and suffered Martha to lead her from the room, without speaking one word or shedding one tear!

It was different with myself. I beheld death for the first time, but it had no terrors for me: living or dead, how could I feel fear from the presence of my father?

I kissed with passionate love his face and

hands. I called frantically on his name, and implored him to look once more on his bereaved and miserable child. I was for the time mad with the dreadful sense of my desolation, and desecrated that awful chamber with my impious ravings. I know not how long I remained alone. It was Mr. Spencer who first entered the room and raised me from the bed.

"You must come with me," said he, gently, but firmly. "Ellen, you must learn to control your feelings. Your mother, I fear, will be for some time wholly incapable of attending to her family. Your helpless sister and young brothers have only you to look to for aid in this time of trouble. Will you selfishly indulge your own grief, instead of endeavouring to alleviate theirs? Show how you loved your father by the manner in which you discharge the duties entailed on you by his death. Go to your mother, and try to rouse her from the dreadful state of apathy into which she has fallen."

Ashamed of the selfish forgetfulness of my duty, I followed Mr. Spencer from the room.

I found my mother seated on a chair by the window; she had neither spoken nor moved since Martha had placed her there. She gazed at me, as I entered, with a troubled look—as if endeavouring to recall to her recollection who I was.

"Dearest mother," said I, "will you come with me to poor Esther's room? she wants you to comfort her in this dark hour."

"Thank you," she replied, "I will go by and by; when he revives. Now it is my duty to be here."

"Oh, Mr. Spencer!" cried I, "can you do nothing to restore her to consciousness?"

"It is better for her as it is," he answered. "I will send a sleeping draught, which you must persuade her to swallow. The strain on the nervous system has been so great, that I fear if she does not procure rest her brain may become permanently injured; and that, Ellen, will be a greater calamity than the death of your father; but go to your sister, and leave Martha to attend to her mistress."

Before I left my mother, I implored her to speak to me. She answered in the same calm tone, "When he revives I will do as you wish, now it is my duty to be here."

As I opened the door of Esther's room, I thought in my heart, was there ever sorrow like my sorrow? My father dead — my mother bereft of reason — my sister a helpless cripple — my brother a miserable outcast — my younger ones with no one but such a feeble guide as myself to look to for help and consolation!

Esther was still in bed: owing to the troubles and duties of that dreadful morning, Martha had been unable to give her customary attendance to the poor girl. Walter and Edmund were with her, and as I entered she was reading to them from the Bible. They were blessed words I heard, as I approached the bed. The poor children had evidently been weeping bitterly, but strove hard to hush their sobs, as their sister, in a low, faltering voice, read to them from the holy volume.

When she closed the book, Edmund's tears

again burst forth, and he cried, "Oh, Nelly! why did papa die and leave us all? What shall we do without him? What shall we do?"

He wrung his hands in passionate excitement as he spoke; and I, fearful his violent emotion would agitate Esther, endeavoured to calm him, by telling him that his father was now in Heaven, that God ordered all things aright, and that it was wicked of him to murmur or repine.

Alas! when did such attempts at consolation succeed in alleviating the violence of natural grief? I should have derived no comfort from them had they been addressed to myself; and how could I hope to impress my brothers with words that would have fallen lifeless on my own ear?

But Esther acted differently, and soothed the grief felt for the loss of one parent by reminding him of the love and duty he owed the other. "You would not do anything which might distress or injure our mother. Go down, dear boy, with Walter, and remain quiet till Nelly or Martha can come to you."

Walter's sorrow was not so demonstrative as his brother's, but I felt sure he suffered more from not giving it expression.

Since I had been in Esther's room, I had internally been accusing her of insensibility to the heavy affliction we had just sustained.

I did not, in my selfishness, reflect how much more she must be suffering, for repressing all outward expressions of her feelings, while endeavouring to comfort her brothers.

But as soon as we were alone the pent-up agony burst forth, and, with a bitter cry, she threw her arms around my neck, and said, "Oh! Nelly you had the blessed privilege of being with him to the last. I would gladly —oh, how gladly!—have given all the remainder of my wretched, useless existence, to have spent the last six days as you have spent them! Oh! my father, my father! that I could see your face once more!"

I was frightened by her violence, and endeavoured in vain to calm her. "Dearest

Esther, for my sake—for my mother's sake—strive to calm yourself. What would she do if you, too, were taken from her!"

"Bear with me for a little time, Nelly—I will try and bury my grief in my own heart; but I felt as if it must burst with the weight of my wretchedness! Now we must both remember how much we have to do for others. You must commence fresh duties at once, and take Martha's place in assisting the poor cripple."

I did all I could to aid my sister, but I was an awkward substitute for her kind and practised nurse. When, by bringing the sofa to the side of the bed, I managed to place her on it, she thanked me with kind and loving words for the help I had given her. Then followed a long and important conversation.

We had but few friends, and but one relative in the world—a maiden sister of my father's, many years older than himself: she had lived with her brother previous to his marriage, and chose to consider herself ill-treated when he brought a more legitimate mistress to his house.

"Ought we to write to Miss Travers"—we never spoke of her as aunt—"and entreat her to come to our assistance?"

Esther decided it would be right to do so; and wrote by that night's post to Clifton, where she resided, acquainting her with the particulars of my father's death, and my mother's incapacity of attending to her family. To that letter we never received a reply.

In the evening, Mr. Lancester brought Henry home. I could not suppress a shudder of horror as he stooped over Esther's couch to caress her. He looked at me with an expression, half of shame, half of defiance, as I drew back when he advanced towards me.

The remorse of which Mr. Lancester had spoken had not lasted long. It was quite evident from his manner that he had ceased to consider himself the cause of his father's death. After he had demanded to see his mother, and I told him it was impossible he could do so, he muttered something about not being wanted there, and suddenly quitted the room.

Mr. Lancester was surprised at his behaviour. He had completely imposed on him by the violence of his grief, when first acquainted with the effects produced by his letter.

But Henry always had the comfortable faculty of throwing off any feeling of compunction which occasionally visited him; and I had no doubt by this time he had completely absolved himself from blame.

CHAPTER V.

Of the week which followed my father's death I will not write. Who is so fortunate as not to know, by bitter experience, the miseries of such a period: the darkened house, the stealthy footsteps, the whispering voices, the glimpses occasionally caught of strange men in shabby suits of black, the smothered tread of the same grim attendants in a house of mourning, as they pass the door of the room where you are weeping, carrying with them that weighty thing, which, senseless as it is, sends a cold shudder to the heart as it gives audible tokens of its presence, carefully as it is taken up the stairs?

I believe all these things are unknown to the rich and great: that fashion carries the living from the abode of the dead; and though they may take sorrow within their hearts, they leave the gloom and outward evidences of its existence to servants and hired mourners.

We tasted the full bitterness of death; and when my father was laid in the grave, and light and sound once more admitted within our dwelling, my heart seemed still more saddened by the contrast they offered to my feelings.

My mother had only partially recovered from the stupor which had followed my father's death. Long and heavy slumbers rendered her for days unconscious of all that passed around her, and to this cause Mr. Spencer said she was indebted for the recovery of her reason.

It was not till the evening following the funeral that she recognised those about her, and even then she did not appear to remember the events which had occasioned her illness.

Long and miserable were the days that followed. I had overcome some of my repugnance to the presence of Henry, and was compelled to agree with Esther that he was of great service to us in taking charge of the boys. He was kind and affectionate in his manner to all, and appeared to regard his mother with passionate attachment: and this apparent affection was a great solace to her, when gradually the recollection of my father's illness and death recurred to her memory.

How thankful I was this consolation was her's: that she knew nothing of the share he had in producing the wretchedness he sought so sedulously to soothe. But my own mistrust of him was still too great to be overcome by his present examplary conduct. I felt confident that the time would arrive when fresh sorrows would assail us through his agency; and, though I strove hard to forgive him, yet I could never forget that my father was stricken to the earth in the act of perusing his cruel letter.

Weeks rolled away, and we had gradually returned to our usual mode of life. My young brothers had returned to school, and I was anxiously hoping that Henry would leave home and resume his duties in the counting house of Mr. Rivers. My mother had become so accustomed to his society, and soothed by the kind caressing manner he adopted towards her, that I for a long time hesitated to remind him of the necessity of his leaving her.

At length I summoned courage to do so. To the dismay of Esther and myself, he answered, "He never intended to return to Liverpool. In fact, if he wished to do so, it was no longer in his power; that some time back Mr. Rivers had written to him, and informed him the situation he had so long neglected was bestowed on another."

This was a misfortune we had not anticipated; the idea of Henry's being always at home idle was dreadful: besides, it was absolutely necessary he should endeavour to support himself, as Mr. Lancester had recently informed me the strictest economy would be necessary if we continued to reside in the house we had so many years inhabited.

My father had been the junior partner in a banking-house in the City, and well knowing how impossible it would be for Henry to succeed him in the firm, he had directed in his will—to which my mother was sole executrix—that his interest in the business should be disposed of, and the sum it realised, as well as all his other property, he bequeathed absolutely to my mother, who, little accustomed to think or act for herself, had entreated Mr. Lancester to arrange her affairs for her to the best of his judgment. This he cheerfully agreed to, and when everything was settled, he had told her that her income would not exceed eight hundred a year. Within this sum, therefore, it was absolutely necessary we should limit our expenses.

Since my father's death, my mother had never atttempted to resume her duties as housekeeper. She left everything to my management, and very great were the anxieties my stewardship occasioned me, as I was not long in discovering that some retrenchment must be made in the household if I intended to keep the promise I had given Mr. Lancester of living within my mother's income.

From my earliest recollection, we had

resided in a large old-fashioned house in the neighbourhood of Streatham Common, which my father had inherited, shortly after his marriage, from an uncle; and if we did not keep so many carriages and servants as some of our wealthy neighbours, we possessed all the comforts and many of the luxuries of life.

Owing to the habitual ill health of my mother, we had but few friends or acquaintance; she was not equal to the fatigue of giving entertainments or of accepting them from others, so that our intercourse with the families in the vicinity was restricted to occasional morning calls, and friendly inquiries and hand-shakings when we met in our walks and drives.

My mother formerly had but one favourite pursuit—her garden: of that she never tired. Whenever the weather would permit, she would occupy herself the greater part of the day in it; and was never so happy, as, when followed by the gardener, carrying his spade or watering-pot, she gave directions for the removal of different plants, or planned alterations in the form or situations of her various flower-beds.

We used, laughingly, to tell her she could find employment for a dozen gardeners if we could afford to keep them, in consequence of the continual improvements her taste or fancy suggested. She always managed that her greenhouse should supply flowers through the winter, so that the vase on Esther's table should never be destitute of beautiful blossoms. It was her one sole pleasure, and happy did we feel, as children, when we were enabled to contribute to it, by the present of some rare plant, or in the early Spring a bouquet of flowers from Covent Garden, choicer than those her own greenhouse would furnish.

Now, though she had lost all interest in her once-loved occupation, the expense attending the garden was as great as ever. Whatever alterations we resolved on, it was decided by Esther and myself that none must take place there.

Very long used to be the conversations between us on the important topic; furnished with paper and pencil, I would sit for hours by the side of my sister's sofa, and put down, item by item, the articles we considered absolutely necessary for the supply of the family, and reckon the sum they amounted to; then we would discover that something must be omitted from the list; and when we again went over it, were obliged to declare it was impossible to do with less.

When Mr. Lancester had first informed us of the amount we should receive yearly, I considered the sum much larger than we need expend. Our monthly bills appeared very moderate in comparison to the income; but I had forgotten the large demands that must be made on it for the expenses of my brothers' education: these were little short of two hundred and fifty pounds yearly; while the servants' wages, including the gardener, were nearly half as much. Then there were heavy bills each Christmas for medical attendance on my mother and sister, and innumerable claims of various descriptions, of which I was ignorant till it became necessary to discharge them.

After all our deliberations, there was only one mode of retrenchment which we mutually agreed might be made without inconvenience to my mother. We could very well dispense with the man-servant, and this would, independent of his wages, materially lessen the household expenditure. Still it was impossible to carry our scheme of economy into action without consulting our mother; and, reluctant as I was to annoy her with details respecting our domestic perplexities, I was obliged to call her attention to them before I considered myself at liberty to remove them.

"Do as you think best, love," was the answer she gave, when I had explained the plan we had devised for "making both ends meet!"

"We must not, of course, spend more than our income. You are very young, Nelly, to have the charge of house and purse—but I have confidence in your prudence, and trust them implicitly to your management."

It was a great comfort to my sister and

myself when we had arranged this difficult affair; but I could not refrain from reflecting how much more easy the task would have been if Henry was maintaining himself by his own industry, instead of encroaching considerably on my mother's very moderate resources.

It was dreadful to see a young man of two-and-twenty, in perfect health, pass his existence in the state of listless idleness that my brother did at this time. He would come down in the morning, hours after the family breakfast was over; daudle over the one prepared for him for more than an hour; and then, if the day was fine, saunter round the garden with his mother for a short time. The remainder of his time he would spend as idly as the morning. He did not seem to possess sufficient energy to care even for his personal appearance, but would most frequently pass the whole day in his morning coat and slippers.

With all his faults, he possessed one good quality in abundance—he was good-tempered. That is, unless he was thwarted in some wish which it was absolutely impossible he could be allowed to gratify without great imprudence.

When we first met in the morning, or parted for the night, his caresses and expressions of affection would have led a stranger to imagine he was the kindest and most devoted of brothers. It was that manner of his that used to irritate me so much against him.

"Seeming, seeming!" I used to exclaim in my heart. I knew, when we separated for the night, that he would not care a straw if we never met again; yet he would not suffer me to leave him till he had kissed me again and again, and again and again repeated his "God bless you, my darling little Nelly!"

I often wondered whether he imposed on himself, whether he really believed he cared for the mother, brothers, and sisters, on whom he bestowed such outward demonstrations of affection; and I verily believe he did. That is, so long as he was with them he thought he was devoted to them all; but leave home for one day, and it was to him only the place from which he was to obtain the means of living in idleness and profligacy.

Unhappy Henry! your life truly exemplified the words, "That to be weak is to be miserable." I believe that you formed good resolutions after you had been rescued from the miseries entailed by your own misconduct, but they were overthrown the moment temptation to evil assailed you.

Esther at this time used to console me for the manner in which his time and energies were wasted, by saying that if at home we should be thankful his presence was a consolation to our mother, and that if he would not contribute to his own maintenance, by procuring some occupation, it was better he should be idle at home, instead of absent. At least, it was a satisfaction to know he was not passing his time viciously.

Two years had elapsed since my father's death, and with so little incident to mark their progress, that I often marvelled at the swiftness with which week succeeded week. The only interruption to our monotonous existence was the return home of Walter and Edmund for their vacations.

Poor children! their holidays were no longer times of pure enjoyment, as formerly. No visits to the theatres in winter; no long walks into the country and games of cricket in the summer. Henry was too indolent to exert himself in any way for their gratification, and my mother's delicate health compelled every one in the house to move quietly and speak softly : great restraints to young, healthy boys, accustomed to the noise and freedom of the school playground.

My mother had never fully recovered from the illness occasioned by the shock of my father's death : sweet-tempered and patient, she yet never appeared to take an interest in the things passing around her, and though, supported on Henry's arm, she would pass some time daily in the garden, she no longer busied herself in its arrangement. It was very, very painful to me to witness the listless manner in which she would walk round the spot which formerly furnished her with such cheerful occupation.

Mr. Spencer, fearful this apathetic state of mind should increase, advised me to try whether a total change of scene might not act beneficially on her nerves.

"Why not," said he, "leave this place, and form a home in some quite fresh locality? Such a course would be likely to rouse her from the state into which she has remained since your father's death better than any other mode I can devise."

I eagerly caught at this suggestion, nor did I anticipate that she would raise an objection to any plan I might propose.

One day, therefore, when walking with her in the garden, after having in vain endeavoured to excite her attention by talking of the flowers and plants she used to love so much, I said, "Dear mamma, I believe we are all tired of this place; suppose we leave it, and try if fresh scenes may not prove beneficial to us all."

To my surprise and grief, she was more agitated than I had seen her since my father's death. She passionately reproached me for wishing to remove her from the home endeared to her by so many associations; and said, that if tired of the monotony of our mode of life, I was at liberty to quit it, and spend my time in any way more congenial to my feelings.

"Oh! Nelly," cried she—while frightened at her vehemence I stood speechless before her—"why will you not allow me to die in peace? If you wish to hasten my death, then insist on my quitting the scene of all the happiness I have ever known, of all the comfort I am now capable of receiving. I cannot, and I will not, abandon to strangers the house in which I gave birth to my children, in which my husband died. Esther and Henry are not tired of it if you are, and they will refuse to join in your cruel scheme for forcing me to leave it."

I did not attempt to justify myself, by saying it was for her sake only I was anxious to quit the home of my youth. I think we all inherited from her a love of locality, a disinclination for change of any kind, but I had caught with avidity at Mr. Spencer's suggestion, in the hope of its benefitting her, and I had only succeeded in inducing her to believe that it was for my own selfish gratification I had proposed to remove from Streatham.

After a few minutes, she resumed her usual gentle and listless manner.

"Forgive me, Nelly, if I have spoken unkindly, but you cannot imagine the shock your proposal gave me. I shudder at the bare idea of leaving this place, and going forth into the world from which I have been so long secluded."

I kissed her with a heart full of contrition for the pain I had unwittingly occasioned her, and from that time Mr. Spencer abandoned the thought of her removal.

Shortly after this attempt to induce my mother to leave Streatham, a new source of uneasiness was awakened in my heart. Henry, who, from the time of his father's death, had never cared to leave the house, now began to absent himself from home. At first he would return at reasonable hours in the evening; but gradually he remained out later and later, and as it was impossible to keep the servants up night after night for the purpose of admitting him, I used to sit in Esther's room, waiting anxiously through the dreary hours for the sound of the opening gate, which told me of his arrival. When this welcome noise met my ears, I would steal softly down-stairs, and have the door opened before he had time to alarm my mother by the sound of bell or knocker.

Usually he was good-tempered when he entered, and would thank me for serving him so quickly; but more than once he was savagely unkind, and accused me of sitting up in order to play the part of a spy on his actions.

One thing was in Henry's favour, the only one which gave me hopes of his reformation —he never debased himself by intoxication. At whatever time he returned home, in whatever society he had passed the hours of his absence, he was always perfectly sober when I admitted him, and though of course I could not know from observation how seldom this was the case with men who behaved as he did, yet I remembered hearing Mr. Lancester, on one occasion, endeavour to comfort my father by the assurance, that so long as that vice was not added to the catalogue of his faults, there was hope he would become sensible of the degrading state to which his conduct frequently reduced him. I was made intensely miserable by the change which had taken place in his behaviour. I was old enough to be aware that he could not lead the life he did without spending considerable sums of money, and though he had not yet applied to his mother for more than a few pounds occasionally, I felt certain that eventually she would be called on to discharge the debts he must be contracting.

Esther, with her usual sunny philosophy, consoled me by saying we must not be very unhappy concerning him, so long as he returned home nightly. But even that miserable comfort was soon taken from us—two nights I watched in vain for his return, and fearful thoughts as to the duration of his absence, and the state in which we might probably discover him, agitated my mind.

I had not long to wait for the cause of his absence. With all my economy, it was a difficult task to do more than make our income suffice for our expenditure, and some money which Henry had recently obtained from his mother had left her with barely five pounds at the bankers when the next quarter's money was paid in.

It was my custom to pay all the household bills monthly, but as Mr. Lancester had told me I should not pay small sums by cheque, I was in the habit of obtaining one with my mother's signature, and filling it up for whatever amount I required, and this was always cashed for me by a tradesman with whom we had dealt for many years. The day following one of those monthly settlements, I was told that Mr. Hunt wished to see me. This was the person who had cashed the cheque for me the day before, for thirty-five pounds. When I entered the dining-room, where he was waiting for me, I perceived, to my great surprise, that he had this cheque in his hand.

"I am sorry to trouble you, miss," commenced he, before I could ask him the reason of his visit, "but I am sure when you asked me to cash this cheque yesterday, you did not know there were no assets at the bank to meet it."

I suppose my looks must have shown the astonishment I felt at his words, for before I could reply to him, he said, "It is no mistake of mine, Miss Ellen, for I took it to Lombard Street myself this morning, and the cashier returned it to me as I have told you."

By this time I had sufficiently recovered from the surprise his first words occasioned me, to assure him it was a mistake, for that the week previously two hundred pounds had been paid to my mother's credit, and that this was the first cheque which had been drawn on it.

"But I will go with you at once," said I, "and have this great error corrected;" and without seeing either Esther or Martha, I left the house with my creditor.

It was with perfect confidence and self-possession that I entered the banking house, and followed Mr. Hunt to that part of the counter where the cheques were received.

"Here is Miss Travers," said he, to the cashier, "come to speak to you about this cheque you returned to me this morning. She says you have two hundred pounds of her mamma's in hand."

"The young lady is mistaken," was the civil reply. "We had something over that sum two days ago—but she had better take the book and look over it, and she will see that the two hundred pounds were drawn out in one cheque."

I stretched out my hand to receive the proffered book, and immediately looked at the last entry it contained. It was to "H. T.—£200."

"Here are the cheques," said the cashier. "The last is for the sum I mentioned, and is dated Wednesday last."

I looked at the paper he held towards me. It was filled up in my brother's hand, and bore the signature of my mother. Completely stunned by this unexpected misfortune, I stepped into the cab which was waiting to convey me home without speaking one word to my civil attendant.

I could not collect my faculties sufficiently to consider the consequences of this cruel conduct of my mother's—that she should, without a word of warning to myself, have parted with every shilling of the money required for our support during the ensuing three months, and that to supply the profligacy of my brother, was a blow so unexpected, that for a time I was completely overwhelmed by it. I was roused from my bitter reflections by the voice of Mr. Hunt.

"Don't be cast down, miss," said the kind-hearted man; "I am in no hurry for my money. I am quite sure you thought it was all right when you asked me to give you the money for the cheque; you are quite welcome to the loan of it till your mamma has made things straight at the bank. It can't be long before a lady like Mrs. Travers will be able to pay such a sum as this."

"You shall be paid this very evening, Mr. Hunt," said I; "and I am indeed sorry you should have to wait till then for the money you advanced me for the cheque."

Not another word was spoken till I returned his civil "good morning" at the door of my mother's house.

Hastening directly to her room, I was welcomed with more emotion than she usually displayed. She was netting, and as I entered she exclaimed, "Oh! Nelly, where have you been? I have wanted you to match this silk I am using for a purse for Henry. The other other day, when I gave him some money, he told me he had nothing to put it in."

My mother looked and spoke as calmly as if it was a commonplace occurrence to give her eldest son every shilling she possessed, and I could not refrain from saying, bitterly, "You must make a larger purse than that, mamma, if Henry wishes it to contain the money you gave him on Wednesday."

She looked up from her work, evidently surprised at the tone in which I had spoken. "I think, Nelly, this will hold all I gave him—ten pounds do not require a very capacious purse to contain it."

As I listened to my mother's words, and saw the perfect unconsciousness she evinced of the amount of the cheque Henry had presented at the bank, the truth flashed instantly across my mind, and I only wondered I had remained so long blind to it. She, as was her invariable habit, had simply signed the cheque, and Henry had taken advantage of her confidence to fill it up for the large sum he had obtained.

Before acquainting her with what I was sure would greatly agitate her, I resolved to consult Esther. She was the consoler and adviser of all my difficulties, and I hoped in the present instance she might devise some scheme by which we could replace the money without my mother having the pain of learning the manner in which it had been abstracted.

I found my sister greatly alarmed at my unusual absence, which she had immediately associated with Henry's disappearance during the last two days. She was soon acquainted with the facts, and I besought her to think of some plan by which this fresh evidence of our brother's unworthiness might be concealed from his mother. To my great surprise, she counselled that she should be immediately informed of it.

"We have no right in any way to procure

money without her sanction, Nelly; besides, I do not see how it is possible we could do so; and the sum you are indebted to Mr. Hunt must be paid immediately. But let us consult Martha, she will judge better than we can how far it may be prudent to acquaint my mother with Henry's conduct."

This faithful confidante was shocked when we communicated to her the events of the morning, and like myself appeared apprehensive of the effects the knowledge of them might produce on my mother; but after a few minutes' consideration, she said, "Miss Esther is right; you are too young to act in this business without my mistress's knowledge; you must tell her of it at once, dear."

"Not alone, Martha," cried I, fearfully. "I could not tell alone; let her come here, and Esther's presence may give me courage to tell her what I am sure will occasion her great sorrow."

"I will find some means of sending her to you at once, then," answered my nurse, and she left the room hastily, as if fearful my resolution would give way if not directly executed.

In a few minutes she returned, accompanied by my mother, who said reproachfully to me, " Nelly, you have forgotten the silk I requested you to find for me, so I have taken Martha's advice, and have come to seek for it myself."

" Sit down, darling mother," said Esther, boldly approaching the subject from which I cowardly shrunk. " Nelly has been out this morning on business, and it is necessary you should know what it was."

My mother looked surprised at this unusual demand on her attention, and in a tone of some annoyance, replied, " I conclude it is nothing but what you are competent to arrange, Nelly."

" My dear mother," said Esther, " cannot you believe that we should not have troubled you by speaking of what could have been settled without consulting you. Nelly is in difficulties respecting money, and you must endeavour to explain to her how she can immediately obtain some." Then, without waiting for my mother to reply to this unexpected intelligence, she proceeded, "The cheque you gave Henry, and which you imagined he would fill up for ten pounds, was in reality drawn for two hundred, and in consequence of this want of thought in my brother, we have no funds at the banker's to meet immediate and pressing demands."

All the time Esther was speaking I had held my eyes fixed on the face of my mother, in the apprehension she would be violently agitated by the intelligence so abruptly communicated to her; but, to my astonishment and delight, she listened to my sister with composure, and when she had ceased speaking, desired, in a calm voice, to be informed of all the particulars respecting the transaction.

I told her as concisely as possible of the visit of Mr. Hunt with the dishonoured cheque, and of my going with him to the bank. I then placed in her hand the banker's book, together with the cheque which had enabled Henry to obtain the money. While my mother listened, a cloud seemed to pass from her face, and it became animated by the look so long missed from it—the look of anxious love it formerly wore when interested in any of the sorrows and anxieties of our daily life.

"My dear children," said she, humbly, when I had concluded my narrative, "I fear I have been greatly to blame. Sunk in selfish apathy since the loss of my husband, I have neglected the duties of a mother, and allowed you, my dear girls, to fight with difficulties which never might have arisen had I exerted myself to act rightly. Had I insisted on Henry's procuring some employment, instead of encouraging him to pass the last two years in such deplorable idleness, he might not again have fallen back into the vices and extravagancies of his earlier years. It was love for me, and the fear that I should mourn his absence, which induced him to resign his situation in the counting house of Mr. Rivers. During the time he was occupied there, not a shadow of misconduct stained his name. True, indeed, are the words of the proverb, 'The busy man has but one devil, the idle man has a hundred.' Alas! that my own sinful indulgence of sorrow should have occasioned the ruin of my son."

Esther and I looked at each other in painful surprise, as we heard our mother accuse herself as the author of Henry's dishonesty. Many times since my father's death had we congratulated each other that she was in ignorance of the share he had in producing that calamity; but now it was with great difficulty I could refrain from informing her of the truth, and thus spare her the bitterness of self-reproach, but Esther gave me a warning look, and I remained silent.

My mother then desired to be made acquainted with all the particulars respecting my brother's late conduct, and when he first began to display the fatal symptoms of his return to his former evil courses.

I told her how, for the last few weeks, he had returned home at all hours of the night, and that for the last two he had absented himself altogether. I then pressed on her attention the necessity for immediately procuring money.

"You need not be uneasy on that point, Nelly," answered she; "I can soon replace the money Henry has stolen from us—yes, stolen from us! Esther, darling, you must not shrink at hearing the true word applied to your brother's unscrupulous conduct. I do not say that legally he could be punished for the theft, for I trusted him to fill up the cheque, but he has taken a base advantage of the confidence reposed in him, to rob me of a sum he well knew I should never have bestowed on him. The unhappy boy is like those men who can abstain altogether from intoxicating liquids, but who cannot partake of them in moderation. He will remain months, and even years, contentedly in seclusion, but once let him put the cup of what he calls pleasure to his lips, and all self-restraint vanishes the moment he tastes the temptation with which it is filled; but now, Nelly, for action. Will you write to our only friend, and ask him to come to us at once?"

I reminded my mother that Mr. Lancester was in Scotland, and added, that had he been at home I should have endeavoured, through his assistance, to have kept her in ignorance of Henry's conduct.

"Then, Nelly, I am glad he is absent. It was a terrible calamity which deprived you so long of a mother's care, and I bless God that even by a fresh sorrow I am awakened to the knowledge of my own sinful repinings at His will; I will pray that strength may be given me to combat with the difficulties which my own neglect of duty has occasioned."

She then directed me to write to the gentleman who for many years had acted as my father's solicitor, and request him to call on her immediately.

To me, the wonderful change which the last hour had wrought in my mother appeared miraculous. The mental lassitude which for the last two years had obscured her intellect was quite dissipated, and when Mr. Bingley arrived, she received him with the greatest composure, and stated, in business-like language, her immediate necessity for three hundred pounds.

This gentleman was perfectly well acquainted with my mother's affairs, and knew exactly the amount of her income, and he looked both surprised and vexed when she concisely mentioned her need of so large a sum.

"Of course, Mrs. Travers," he replied, "you can directly have any sum you may require, your late husband's will gives you the power of disposing as you please of the property he bequeathed you, but you must pardon me for observing that it is usually a dangerous expedient to encroach on the capital of the money from which your income is derived, and I must advise you, as a friend, to be very careful how you incur the necessity of doing so. If Mr. Lancester were in town, he might, perhaps, persuade you to relinquish your intention of doing so now."

My mother was evidently pained by the grave manner in which Mr. Bingley remonstrated with her. It was easy to discover that he considered her conduct most imprudent, but it was impossible to exculpate herself from the charge without denouncing the conduct of her son.

When he found she persisted in her resolution of procuring the money, he promised to send a cheque for the amount to the bank directly.

"It is very easy for you, my dear Mrs. Travers," said this kind and prudent friend, as he took his leave, "to sign your name and transfer your property to other persons, but I must again warn you of the peril of so doing, and sincerely hope you will not a second time require my services for such a purpose."

CHAPTER VI.

Henry did not give us a long respite. Before three weeks had elapsed from the time of his obtaining the money, he returned home, but this time he did not, as was usually the case after one of his transgressions, appear penitent and humble; he was not absent long enough to experience privation, and it was with the air of one who had received an injury rather than committed it, that he made his appearance late one afternoon in Esther's room, where my mother and myself were sitting.

As his mother rose to receive him, he looked at her with amazement; he perceived in a moment that a great change had passed over her since he had last seen her, and the sullen, defiant look, with which he had entered, was changed to one of shame and apprehension as she said, "I must speak to you, but not here; go down, and I will join you in a few minutes."

When he had obeyed her command, she said, with a sad voice, "I must do my duty, painful though it be; to-night must decide whether I am still to regard Henry as a son whom I can admit to associate with my other children. If he can give no satisfactory explanation of his absence, and the purpose for which he obtained that money, I will not suffer him to be an inmate of my house."

I could not avoid feeling as if my mother committed an injury against her other children, by hinting at the possibility of Henry's being able to exculpate himself in any way from the charge of having basely defrauded her of the money from the banker's. Truly she was one who could pardon the offences of this best loved of her children, not seven times only, but seventy times seven.

I never knew what passed between them in that interview, but after it had lasted more than two hours, they returned together to Esther's room. My mother's face betrayed signs of violent emotion, but Henry's still wore the same half-ashamed, half-defiant expression with which he had quitted the room.

"My dear children," said my mother, with a voice in which sorrow and joy seemed mingled, "welcome Henry home; this night has, I hope, restored to you a brother I feared you had for ever lost. To-morrow you shall hear the plans he has formed for his future life, and I have promised to assist him to the utmost of my ability in carrying them into execution."

Very shortly after, Henry, on the plea of fatigue, wished us good night, and retired to his room. My dear mother's eyes followed him with an anxious, troubled look, though she had endeavoured to appear tranquil, and even cheerful, while he remained in the room.

"I am thankful to have your brother once more under this roof, Nelly," said she, in answer to some question I had put to her relative to his absence. "He has promised amendment, and told me the money he obtained by such unjustifiable means was to satisfy claims of long standing, and which, if he had not discharged at the moment he did, would have rendered him liable to disgrace and imprisonment."

The following day we were made acquainted with Henry's wishes for his future career. He was anxious to emigrate to one of our colonies, and my mother had promised to consult Mr. Lancester on the subject as soon as he returned to town, on the best mode of enabling him to establish himself respectably either in Canada or Australia.

"A few days ago," said his poor mother, "I should have looked on his departure from England as the greatest misfortune which could have occurred to me; now I view it as the only hope of his salvation. Removed from the pernicious influence of his old companions, and placed with those ignorant of his past excesses, he may, with God's blessing, lead a new life, and return to us at some future day a son and a brother we may welcome with love and esteem. It will take a large sum, I fear, to give him this chance of reformation, but I am sure you can all bear cheerfully any deprivations when they may be compensated for by the blessed hope of a brother's redemption from sin."

Henry remained at home three days, nor did he attempt to leave the house once during that period, but his mind was evidently preoccupied, and his manner constrained and gloomy. He appeared to be always in a state of expectation; every ring at the bell agitated him, and he always loitered near the hall door at the time the postman was in the habit of leaving letters. Once or twice during the three days he took them himself from the man, and after their perusal became still more restless and unhappy.

Late in the evening of the third day there was a loud peal of the gate bell, and a servant entered almost immediately, and said a person was waiting outside to speak with Mr. Henry. Without speaking a word, my brother rushed from the room, and the next instant we heard the street door close after him.

For several hours we listened anxiously for his return, but when one o'clock struck, and he was still absent, Martha succeeded in persuading my mother to retire, as it was not probable " Mr. Henry would come home that night." I believed he would, and determined to watch, as I had done so frequently of late, at the window of the room which overlooked the small shrubbery which surrounded the house. The night was dark, but a gas lamp over the front gate gave sufficient light to enable me to discern any one approaching the door.

I had waited more than an hour, when I heard, as I thought, the footsteps of more than one person pause at the gate. After a short interval it was opened, and, to my great relief, I saw Henry advance alone towards the house. When I admitted him he appeared in high spirits, thanked me for sitting up for him, and said he hoped there was something in the house he could have for supper, as he was very hungry. I told him there was wine and biscuits in the dining-room.

"That will not do," he answered. "Run down to the kitchen, there's a good child, Nelly, and see what you can find for me, I will fasten the door," and taking the chain from my hand, he almost pushed me towards the kitchen stairs.

While I was in the pantry, I fancied I heard the street door again opened; and fearful he was about to leave the house, I called out "I shall be up directly, Henry; pray, pray do not go out again to-night." But at that instant my fears on this point were set at rest, by hearing him bolt and lock the door with a great deal of unnecessary noise.

He then descended to the pantry, and offered to assist me in taking up his supper. I was about to cut some slices from a piece of cold beef when he joined me, but he snatched up the large dish in which it was placed, and saying he was hungry enough to eat the whole of it, carried it up-stairs, I following with the tray containing bread and other articles.

As I deposited it on the dining-room table, he exclaimed, in the same hurried manner, "Now, Nelly, look alive!—give me the key of the plate cupboard, to get a fork and spoons, while you go and draw me some beer."

I did as he desired me, and, after giving

him the key, once more went down the kitchen stairs.

The plate-cupboard was a large closet in the dining-room, such as are frequently met with in old-fashioned houses. It was of sufficient dimensions to admit of three or four persons standing in it at the same time; and from my earliest recollection, it was customary to deposit in it nightly the basket containing the plate used during the day: the door of this closet was strongly plated with iron, and the key never entrusted to any one but Martha or myself.

I believe these precautions were taken in consequence of our being richer in plate than most families in our rank of life. My mother had inherited a considerable quantity of old-fashioned silver from a relative, which, as it was never required for use, was kept in two large chests in the closet I have mentioned.

When I returned to the dining-room with the beer, Henry looked up from his plate, and throwing me the key across the table, said, "I have locked the closet, Nelly, and will turn down the gas in the hall, and see all is right before I go up-stairs, so you had better get to bed at once!"

This proposal excited a vague kind of apprehension in my mind. It was always my custom to remain below till he went to his own room; and I felt instinctively that he had some motive for wishing me to leave him there. I, therefore, answered that I was not sleepy, and should remain till he was ready to accompany me up stairs.

He raised his eyes from his plate, and cast a quick, suspicious glance at my face; then instantly lowered them, and said, sullenly, "Just as you please; only don't look like a martyr to-morrow from headache, and tell every one it is because I kept you up so late."

He appeared for some minutes wholly occupied with his supper, and when he had finished, he said, "I have mislaid my cigar-case, and think it must be in the garden-room; will you hold a candle, while I search for it?"

I immediately followed him to the door of the room he had mentioned, and held the light while he unfastened it. This door was always strongly secured at night, in consequence of an attempt some years previously to obtain an entrance into the house through the window which looked into the garden.

This room was used as a receptacle for all descriptions of litter; anything that had to be put out of the way, any stray article, which had no particular place assigned to it, was thrown into the garden-room: shawls, hats, boots, umbrellas, parasols, the light tools my mother used to use in the garden, Henry's great coats, morning-gowns, and slippers—everything, in short, which went by the name of "litter" was thrust into it; and, therefore, I was not surprised that Henry should think of looking there for his cigar-case.

I held the candle while he hunted on the shelves, searched pockets, and opened drawers; still the missing article was not discovered. After some minutes spent in that manner, he said, " Perhaps, after all, it is in the drawer of the hall-table—wait here a moment while I look."

My back was towards the door as he

quitted the room, but I turned quickly round, when I heard it, as I thought, bolted from the outside. I rushed to it, and found that I was indeed a prisoner. I called loudly to Henry to release me—thinking he had fastened it in sport—but received no reply to my entreaties. He had evidently left the spot.

I was so astonished at the situation in which I found myself, that I could not for some time imagine the reason for such conduct; but the idea suddenly occurred to me that Henry must have some powerful motive for thus securing me. But what could it be? If he had wished to leave the house I could not have prevented him. He was at liberty to act as he pleased. I tried in vain to find a motive for his cruelty; and at last came to the conclusion that it was an ill-natured mode of punishing me for refusing to go to bed when he wished me.

Satisfied that no other motive could have actuated him, my thoughts turned towards my mother. How alarmed she would be if, as was frequently the case, she required my services during the night. Surely, surely Henry would soon release me—he could not be so cruel as to keep me shut in that cold dreary room throughout the night.

I walked impatiently backwards and forwards in my cage; each time pausing at the door to listen for the footsteps of my jailor. But in vain did I expect him! What was I to do? If I screamed loud enough to be heard in the upper part of the house, I should alarm my mother fearfully. No; that was not to be thought of, even if I remained till morning in the prison into which I had been so shamefully entrapped. But could I not devise some method for my release? The window—was it not possible to escape by that? It was very easy to reach from within, but then on the other side was a deep brick area. True, it was not enclosed by railings, but how was I to climb from it to the garden? And even if I succeeded in doing so, how was I to obtain admittance into the house without alarming its inmates? Still anything was better than inaction; only let me escape from the room, and I might be able to think of some mode by which I could enter the house.

With considerable difficulty, I managed to remove the heavy bars with which the shutters were secured; and opening the window, I, by the aid of a chain, easily stepped into the area. The night was densely dark, but, by the faint glimmer of the candle within the room, I could see the top of the brickwork, which I must surmount before I could obtain my freedom. Fruitless were all my efforts to do so; many times I made frantic exertions to raise myself to a level with the garden, and each time I fell back exhausted by my vain endeavours. I was as fast a captive as when I stood within the room itself. I could find no resting-place for my foot in the firm brickwork, and could not spring high enough to place my hands on the top of it.

Hopeless of escape, I sunk to the bottom of the cold, damp area, and burst into tears. It was frightful to be in such a place, at such an hour, without hope of liberation. The wind howled mournfully as it swept over me, while the tall branches of a large acacia tree, which stood close by the window, waved over my head, with a heavy swinging motion, as if they were threatening to strike me. Ah! thought I—as I almost felt them touch me—if I could but manage to clutch you, I might swing myself out of this dreadful place; then the idea flashed across my mind, might I not do so if elevated a little from the ground; could I not drag a chair through the window, and, by standing on it, snatch at the branches as they blew towards me, and by their aid raise myself to the garden.

As soon as I thought of this plan, I hastened to execute it, and, to my great joy, succeeded in dragging the chair through the window, and, standing on it, seized one of the boughs, and in a few seconds I was extricated from my brick prison.

As soon as my feet touched the ground, I stole softly round to the front of the house. I could see through the large old-fashioned fanlight over the door that the gas was still burning in the hall, and this encouraged me to hope that Henry was still in the dining-room. I was about to knock at the window for admission, when I noticed, to my great surprise, that the door was not quite closed. Imagining I must be mistaken, I placed my hand against it. It yielded to the slight pressure, and the next instant I stood within the hall.

The first idea that suggested itself was, that Henry had left the house, and had neglected to shut the door.

The next moment my heart was filled with terror. I fancied I heard the murmur of voices proceeding from the dining-room. An instant I remained irresolute; and then—for nothing is so rash as fear—I opened the door, and stood on the threshold of the room.

What a sight did I behold! Henry was seated on the sofa, and by his side, with her arms encircling his neck—was a woman, who, even in that dreadful moment, I could discern was young and beautiful. The room was in great confusion, the door of the plate closet was wide open, and within stood a man occupied in placing the content of the chests in a large dark sack.

All this was revealed to me in a second, and I conclude I must have uttered some exclamation as I gazed; for, at the same instant, the man's head was turned towards me, and Henry, springing from the sofa, cried, "In God's name! how came you here, Nelly?"

I could not answer; I felt that my lips moved, but no sound escaped them. Henry looked frightened, and moved towards me, when the woman said, in a low, hissing voice, "So, this is Nelly, the spy—is it? that you told me was securely locked up for the night? What did you mean by telling me such a vile falsehood? Did you hope by it to save your mother's plate from the melting-pot? No, no, Master Harry, neither that nor you will escape me this night!"

As she spoke, she rushed to the spot where I stood, and seizing my arm, dragged me to the table, on which stood the tray I had placed for Henry's supper. She took a knife from it, and, turning towards me, said, in a low, distinct voice, "If you make as much noise as a pin would in falling to the ground, I will drive this to your heart!

Ask your brother if I do not know how to use such a weapon when I wish to punish a traitor?"

Still unable to articulate a word, I feebly endeavoured to extricate myself from her firm grasp, but desisted, as she raised the knife with a threatening gesture, and whispered, "Be still, you fool, if you do not wish me to use it!"

Then turning to the man in the closet, she said, "Now, Jasper, have you almost finished?"

"Yes," was the answer; "I have, and pretty heavy the plunder is, too. You and Henry must both help me to carry it to the cab."

"I shall not leave my hold of this girl," said the woman, "till I know you are safely off with the plate. Go and help him, Henry; and when you return I will be ready to join you."

Henry's face was pale and agitated. I could see there was a terrible struggle in his mind as he heard the words of the beautiful demon who held me in such an iron grasp.

He appeared to hesitate as to whether he should obey her commands or hasten to my rescue; but, alas! the evil prevailed over the good in his heart, and, after a moment's irresolution, he took his hat and prepared to quit the room.

Then terror and despair restored to me the power of utterance, and I screamed, "Oh! Henry, my brother! do not leave me with this fearful woman. She will kill me!",

At this instant I received a violent blow on the back of my head, and fell senseless to the ground.

CHAPTER VII.

When I regained consciousness, I was in my own bed; my mother was standing by my side, and Esther reclining on a sofa at the foot. Astonished at beholding her there, I endeavoured to raise myself in the bed for the purpose of asking an explanation of such a remarkable circumstance.

My mother gently replaced my head on the pillow, and said, "Hush, Nelly darling, don't try to speak. God be praised that you know us again! With His blessing you will soon be well. But you must ask no questions yet; when able to do so, you will have much to hear and to relate concerning this dreadful illness."

I soon discovered I had no strength to dispute her commands. Feeble and helpless as an infant, I remained for many days after I was conscious of what passed around me. I laid perfectly quiet; taking the food and medicines which were given me, but without strength or energy to speak one word to those who night and day attended me with such love and care. I remained for hours with closed eyelids, apparently insensible of all outward occurrences; but my mind was slowly recalling the events of that terrible night. Piece by piece they returned to my memory: Henry's return—his locking me in the garden-room—my escape—the horrid scene in the dining-room—and the cruel blow which had felled me to the ground: all rose to my recollection. Then I wondered whether my mother knew the cause of what she had called "my dreadful illness," whether Henry was at home, and most of all was I anxious to know how long a time had elapsed since those events took place.

It seemed as if I must have been long insensible, for it was November when Henry left the house that fatal evening, and now, on the table in my room, stood a vase filled with sprigs of holly, laden with crimson berries, while among them glittered the delicate white blossoms of the Christmas rose. Was it possible that the blessed season, of which they were the symbols, could be nigh at hand, and that weeks had passed while I lay suffering from the effects of that cruel blow?

It was even so. When able to question my mother on the subject, I heard that Christmas had come and passed whilst I remained insensible of all around me, and that on the morrow a new year would commence. Gradually I learnt from my mother and Martha the circumstances which followed the night of the robbery. Not a suspicion of the truth was entertained. When the servants entered the dining-room in the morning I was discovered dead, as they imagined, on the ground—while every article of plate had been removed from the closet; the hall-door was wide open, and it was supposed that hearing footsteps on the gravel in front of the house, I must have concluded Henry was waiting for admission, and that on opening the hall-door the thieves rushed in and struck me down as I fled into the dining-room.

"The only thing the police could not understand," said my mother, "was that, though the front door was open, the robbers appeared to have escaped through the window of the garden-room; and they concluded they must have had a boy with them, as a chair was placed in the area for the purpose of enabling him to reach the garden."

When my mother had finished her recital, she asked me whether the conjectures of the police were correct, and if the thieves had obtained entrance through my mistaking their footsteps for those of my brother.

I knew not what to reply. The supposition was such a very probable one, that I was not surprised it had obtained general credence. Ought I to betray the real culprit, and thus wound my poor mother's heart with the knowledge that her idolized son was the midnight robber of her property, the friend and associate of the base ruffian whose hand had so nearly deprived me of life?

My mother imagined my silence proceeded from exhaustion, and tenderly kissing me, said, "We will talk of that terrible night no more, Nelly. You are mercifully spared to me, and all else is as dust in the balance."

One thing I must know. Had Henry been at home during my illness? I heard, to my great astonishment, that he returned two days after the robbery. That he had read in the papers all the particulars respecting it, and of my dangerous condition. He had taken very active steps, I was told, to discover the thieves, and had the walls in the neighbourhood placarded with bills, containing large offers of reward for their apprehension.

I listened to this account of his behaviour with feelings impossible to describe. That he should add atrocious falsehood to atrocious crime was not surprising, but that fears for his own safety had not deterred him from venturing to pollute his mother's house with his vile presence, that he had not dreaded I should denounce him as the companion and assistant of the midnight robber of her property, did indeed astonish me.

It was with trembling anxiety as to the answer I might receive, that I inquired if he was still at home; to my great relief I was informed he had departed the very evening of the day on which I regained consciousness.

"But don't think him unkind, Nelly," said my mother; "it was affection for you that detained him here so long. It was dreadful to witness his agony during the wretched days we watched over you, every moment fearing you would be taken from us, without one word or look of recognition. As soon as Mr. Spencer had told us the danger was passed, and that you would shortly be able to acquaint us with all the particulars respecting the robbery, your brother quitted the house, nor has he returned since; and, Nelly, my darling child, in the joy of your blessed restoration, I have been too happy to feel anxious on account of his protracted absence."

I was very thankful to hear there was no

probability of my being compelled to meet Henry. At that time I do not believe I could have done so without betraying his guilty knowledge of that night's occurrence.

And for the sake of mother, sister, and brothers, I resolved, if possible, to conceal it. When questioned concerning the appearance of the burglars, I said, with perfect truth, that I could not think of the moment I perceived them without horror, and implored that the subject might never be mentioned to me more. And, in compliance with my entreaties, no allusion was ever made to them in my presence.

I did not gain health and strength as quickly as Mr. Spencer had induced my mother to believe. Winter had passed away, and when the bright sun and warm showers of April arrived, clothing every tree and plant with verdure, and filling the air with delicious odours, I was still that most wretched and helpless of human beings —a nervous invalid.

My days were spent in constant apprehension of evil, my nights in sleepless terror;

every footstep on the stairs caused my heart to beat with frightful violence; and at night, ever before my eyes, was the figure of that dreadful woman, with the knife uplifted to strike me; while the voices of her companion and my brother whispered to me from every corner of the room.

Sometimes, unable to control my fears, I would call to my mother, and implore her to protect me from the forms my imagination had conjured around me.

Alarmed by my cries, she would pass hours by my side, vainly endeavouring to soothe my fears—fears for which she was utterly unable to account.

The impossibility of confiding my horrible secret to any one increased the burthen of my wretchedness. But to whom could I do so? My mother and sister must never know it, or their lives would be rendered as miserable as my own. I could not endure the thought of imparting it to our only friend, Mr. Lancester, for I knew he still regarded Henry with affectionate interest, and that he was in the habit of alleviating my mother's fears on his account, by prognosticating that the son of such an honourable father could not be irreclaimably vicious. This consolation must be lost if he knew the true history of that dreadful night. No; the secret must remain festering in my own heart, poisoning each moment of my life with its fatal venom!

My mother had appeared to gain new life and energy from the commencement of my illness. I never knew her so strong in health or so brave in spirit as during the months I was such a grievous charge to her. Her solicitude on my account never slumbered; no persuasions could induce her to entrust the task of attending me, night or day, to another. I used to lie and watch with wonder her quick, but noiselesss, movements about the room. She never appeared weary; never inattentive to my slightest wish. With what a look of love would she implore me to partake of the delicate nourishment she had prepared for me with such care.

And I did try, for her dear sake, to swallow a portion of what she held to my lips. But

I derived no benefit from doing so; my heart was sick unto death, and no one but myself knew the secret of my fatal malady.

And yet there was one of those who watched over me with such anxious care, who entertained some suspicion of the truth. Martha, my dear old friend—the consoler and *confidante* of every trouble I had ever known—had discovered that my sickness appertained more to the mind than body.

One morning early in May my mother was persuaded to leave me for half an hour, for the purpose of walking round the garden, and Martha was to remain with me during her absence; for since my illness even Esther was neglected. No sooner were we alone, than affectionasely taking my hand, she said—

"My dear Miss Nelly, when you were a little child I remember your telling me the story of the boy who stole a fox and hid it in the bosom of his dress, and though it bit the flesh from his breast, he would not cry out, and thus betray he was the thief. Now you have a secret constantly gnawing at your heart, and, like the boy, you will not cry, lest the thief should be discovered. Tell me, dear child, is not your old nurse right?"

I looked in her kind face and saw that she had not spoken at random; that cautious as I had been, she had divined the cause of my wretchedness; and, by degrees, I confided to her all the particulars of that memorable night.

When I had concluded, and lay sobbing and exhausted in her arms, she said, "Thank you, Miss Nelly; now I shall be able, I hope, to find the means of curing you."

"Say nothing, nurse," cried I, in alarm, "to my mother or Esther! They must never, never know what I have just confided to you."

"Don't fear, my dear, you may safely trust me; but here comes your mamma. Don't you think, ma'am, Miss Ellen looks all the better for her little gossip with me? You feel better, don't you, dear?"

Yes, I certainly did not feel so miserable; the sympathy of one who loved me had lightened my heart of part of the heavy load that had so long burthened it, and my nervous apprehensions in some degree vanished from the time I could confide them to another.

A few days after this conversation with my nurse, my mother said to me, "Do you remember, Nelly, once speaking to me of the benefit we might all derive from leaving this place, and forming a home amidst fresh scenes. I was very unkind to you when you proposed it, but I have for some time past seen the wisdom which dictated it. We will try your scheme at once, my dear, and see whether it may not be the means of bringing back your health and spirits. You will, I hope, revive under the healthful influence of novelty, as my sick plants do when transferred into fresh earth."

I was so astonished at my mother's words, so overpowered by the blessed hope they conveyed to my heart, that I was for some time incapable of replying. To leave the place where I had suffered such fearful sorrow, to be able to live without dreading that each moment might bring fresh calamity, to pass the days in tranquillity and the nights without terror, was a vision of such happiness, that no wonder I was unable to speak to the dear mother who proffered me these blessings. Too soon, alas! was it dispelled. The remembrance of her former dread of removal recurred to my memory, and, ungrateful that I was, the words she had uttered when sick and in misery now seemed to ring in my ears—" If you, for your own selfish reasons, wish to leave us—go."

" No, mamma," answered I, after a long silence, " we will never leave this place; I know your love of it, and that it is only anxiety on my account which induces you to entertain the idea of quitting it. I should indeed be *selfish*, if I allowed you to act in a way so repugnant to your own feelings." I spoke the word *selfish* with some bitterness, and my mother noticed it.

" It is true, my dear child, your mother was most selfish and unjust to you at the time I perceive you remember so well; forgive her all that is past, and trust to her love and care for the future. We will go, Nelly, at least for a time—I cannot even now resolve to abandon this home for ever. We will do so for twelve months, and at the expiration of that period we may, with God's blessing, return to it stronger in health and happier in mind than we leave it. Esther knows of my resolution, and is looking forward with delight to the prospect of beholding a new scene, though only from the window of her chamber."

Ashamed of the ungracious manner in which I had received the first intimation of her intention, I was now eager to express my deep sense of her kindness, but she would not suffer me to do so.

"You have nothing to thank me for, dear; you are to have your share of trouble in this business. Esther and I have resolved that you are to be our director, and we will start under your guidance as soon as you have given us the *route*. Now think where you would like best to spend the next twelve months, for you alone are to decide that important point."

Months after, and when I had perfectly regained health, I knew that Martha was the originator of this scheme—that in conjunction with Mr. Spencer she had induced my mother to propose this step for my restoration — and well did it succeed. A fresh channel was opened for the employment of my thoughts, and they turned towards it with as much avidity as persons rush into pure air after long confinement in a close and polluted atmosphere. It was true we were to return to Streatham, but to a girl of sixteen a year seemed a period of indefinite extent, and therefore the enjoyment of the present was undisturbed by thought of the future.

My mother and sister playfully resisted all my artful endeavours to gain some intimation of their wishes respecting the locality of our new residence.

"It must not be very distant, Nelly," said the former, "that is my only stipulation. Mr. Spencer is to procure an invalid's travelling carriage, in which will be a swinging couch for Esther. She can be placed on it in her own room, and thus be carried to the vehicle; but even in such a conveyance he considers she will not be equal to more than two days' journey, so I fear I must restrict your limits to within fifty miles."

Fifty miles! what an expanse for my imagination to stray over; its very magnitude puzzled me the more. I could have named many charming places within a dozen miles, but when I heard of fifty, I could not fix on one which appeared suitable. Brighton was too hot in summer, and too cold in the early spring; Hastings was beyond the proscribed distance, and Worthing was open to the same objections as Brighton. But because we were to be so far from London, was it necessary to choose any place on the coast? I knew nothing of the country—of the beautiful and quiet hamlets and villages which were scattered within that distance of London. Why, Brookfields did not exceed it! and the letters of Mrs. Hurst, my late governess, were full of descriptions of the beautiful and picturesque scenery of that neighbourhood! Why not write and consult her on the momentous subject? I would do so at once, and the first fruits of my awakened energy was a long letter to this dear friend.

I have not before mentioned our governess, who had left us a short time previous to my father's death, and though we all rejoiced in her present happiness, yet we deeply regretted the loss of her society.

Neither Esther nor myself had ever been separated a day from our parents. My father had an insuperable aversion to ladies' schools. He always said, that though girls might acquire accomplishments, they were never really educated in such establishments, that mental culture was wholly overlooked, while the fingers were kept laboriously occupied either on the keys of a piano, or in producing drawings, which, when elaborately finished off by the skilled hand of the drawing-master, were sent to the parents as evidences of the pupil's improvement.

I was seven years old when my mother was fortunate enough to secure the services of an amiable and accomplished woman as our governess. Dearly did we all love Miss Pritchard, and when she quitted us to fulfil an engagement formed some years before she entered our family, and become the mistress of a pretty parsonage in Berkshire, I was selfish enough to repine at our own deprivation.

Since her marriage, Mrs. Hurst had corresponded regularly with my sister and myself, and I knew how delighted my mother would be if we could obtain our temporary home in the neighbourhood of this beloved friend.

I did not receive an answer to my letter as speedily as I expected, but when it did arrive its contents amply compensated for the delay.

"My Dear Nelly—You ask me where you had better choose a home for the next twelve months. The answer is ready for you—come here. By great good fortune there is a pretty house and garden quite ready for your reception, about a mile from the Vicarage. It is pleasantly situated, and, as I have often told you, the neighbourhood is singularly picturesque.

"I delayed replying to your letter till I had secured the place for you; you are therefore at liberty to take possession of 'Oakdens' in a fortnight from this day, and I will take care that everything is ready to receive you.

"Now, Nelly, you cannot object to this

arrangement. I do not trouble you with the business details, they are such as I am sure Mrs. Travers will approve. Any things which may arrive previous to yourselves I will see properly bestowed. Write and tell what day I may expect to welcome you here, and believe I am

"Ever, dear Nelly,

" Your affectionate friend,

" CATHERINE HURST."

My mother and Esther were quite as much delighted as I expected, when acquainted with the contents of this letter. To reside near Mrs. Hurst was a pleasure which I trusted would compensate, in some degree, to the former, for the sacrifice she made of her own wishes in quitting home for my benefit. Esther loved her as dearly as I did, and even Henry respected her so much that he would listen with patient attention to the affectionate remonstrances she occasionally addressed to him, and would be ashamed to meet her when he returned home after one of his transgressions.

During the fortnight which preceded our departure from Streatham, I regained strength so quickly, that I was able to sit up for a few hours daily in my sister's room, to which Martha used to carry me—her great baby, she used laughingly to call me, as she deposited me in a large chair by the side of my sister's sofa. There I would sit, talking of the new life which was soon to open for us, and watching with admiration her busy fingers as they fashioned lace and muslin into the quaint, neat caps which shaded the kind face of my dear, kind nurse, who never wore any but those Esther manufactured for her. Then my mother would come to us, and consult on various household matters relative both to the home we were quitting and the one we were soon to enter.

It was arranged that Susan, who had lived several years with us, should be left in charge of the house, and that her father, who was the gardener, was to sleep in it during our absence. Should Henry return, she was to provide everything necessary for his comfort, and immediately to apprise Mr. Lancester of the fact, but she was strictly enjoined to give him no clue to our new residence. This my mother was with great difficulty brought to agree to.

Why should not her son join his family when he again wished to form a part of it? But Mr. Lancester was firm in his resolve that my brother should be kept in ignorance of our abode till he had seen him, and discovered how, and with whom, he had passed the time since he had quitted his home.

This circumstance was a great blessing to me. I seemed to breathe new life with the knowledge that he could not, without my being warned of his approach, enter our new home, and carry desolation and misery with his presence. I always thought it was some hint from Martha which caused Mr. Lancester to resist my mother's wishes on this point, and I was very grateful for the wisdom shown by her in giving it.

It was a lovely evening, on the second day after our departure from Streatham, that we arrived at Brookfields. Esther had borne the journey bravely, and I had gathered health and cheerfulness with every mile that we travelled, but my mother, now that the necessity for exertion was over, looked worn and unhappy, and I knew that, much as she loved Esther and myself, she would have preferred remaining solitary at home, awaiting Henry's return.

CHAPTER VIII.

A MONTH after my arrival at Brookfields, I was perfectly well. It was no physical malady which had retarded my progress to health. It was the secret dread of Henry's returning as a thief in the night, bringing with him that fearful woman, which occasioned me to remain for months a wretched, nervous creature; and when, thanks to Mr. Lancester's wise precautions, this terrible fear was removed, I recovered health and spirits in a marvellous manner.

I have never known such perfect happiness as that I experienced during the first weeks of our residence at Brookfields. No one but those who have lived for years in the constant anticipation of some great and sudden calamity, and then, like me, been unexpectedly relieved from the dread of its appearance, can appreciate the blessed feelings of peace and security I now enjoyed.

But this brightness was not destined to continue. It was not long before I saw with dismay that my mother was drifting slowly, but surely, back into the listless melancholy from which Henry's misconduct and my illness had roused her. The necessity for exertion past, she no longer appeared to take interest in anything around her.

Alarmed at this threatened evil, I consulted our friend, Mrs. Hurst, on the painful subject, and entreated her to devise some method of arresting its approach.

"She must have some occupation provided for her mind, Nelly," was the answer I received. "You have told me that you had never known her either so well or cheerful as during the time you required her constant attention. Does not that fact point out what remedies must be applied now? I do not wish you to be ill again in order to supply healthful employment to her mind, but it is essential some means should be devised to interest it. Her thoughts, I believe, are wholly occupied with the past and future —of the one she cannot reflect without sorrow, on the other without apprehension. We must get her to live in the present; and I will consult with one whom you know I consider the wisest of mankind, how this may be best accomplished."

I have not yet spoken of Mr. Hurst. I know not indeed how to convey a faint idea of his character.

At the time we arrived at Brookfields he was forty-six years of age; tall, athletic, and, to my idea, the very handsomest man I had ever beheld. Yet, when I confided my opinion respecting his personal appearance to his wife, she laughingly replied—

"Handsome! Why, Nelly, he has not a good feature in his face!"

I did not attempt to dispute this assertion. I only knew that he had the kindest and brightest of blue eyes, and that his smile was the sweetest, and the expression of his face the most benevolent I had ever gazed on.

He was the kindest, the most patient, the least selfish of human beings. Malevolence itself could not throw one shaft from its poisoned quiver at Philip Hurst. Even the poor people in the village, those most inveterate of grumblers, used to declare that "The very sight of t' parson did 'em good," when sickness or want of employment deprived them of the power of working for their daily bread.

But the Vicar was a stern reprover of the vices of his parishioners: the poacher, the drunkard, the Sabbath-breaker, were not allowed to sin in ignorance of their guilt. Undeterred by dangers, undaunted by difficulties, would that zealous servant of God endeavour to bring the erring members of his flock to the paths of honest labour; and when, by kindness, by persuasion, by untiring love and charity, he succeeded, how did the heart of the good shepherd rejoice over those he had brought into his fold.

Yet Mr. Hurst was nothing of an ascetic; he thought, with Cowper, "that true piety was cheerful as the day." He was a promoter of all harmless merriment; a great advocate for cricket matches, harvest suppers, and school festivals: and at all such rustic gatherings the parson's happy laugh was sure to be heard, the parson's benevolence sure to be exercised. The neighbouring clergy used to whisper among themselves that Hurst was a great deal too lax in his parish, a great deal too familiar with the labouring classes; that it was carrying humility a little too far to stop and shake the hands of all the sick and aged poor whom he met in his walks or rides; and that a man might be a very good Christian without exactly speaking to a pauper as if he was an equal.

Brookfields was the native place of Mr. Hurst: he had been born in the Vicarage, where, for more than fifty years, his father had resided. For some years before his death, the venerable pastor had been unable to perform the duties of his sacred office. His son —an only child—officiated as his curate, and, by his love and devotion, cheered the declining years of the good man's life. When he died, a memorial was addressed to the dean and chapter of the diocese, who had the disposal of the vacant benefice, praying it might be bestowed on the son of the late vicar.

This petition was signed by nearly all the inhabitants of the parish: rich and poor were alike anxious it should be granted.

Philip Hurst was ignorant of the measures taken by the parishioners for his benefit; and it was with feelings of wonder and delight he received the intimation that he was the new vicar of Brookfields.

Now the hope of twelve long years might be realised, and he was in a position to claim Jane Pritchard as a wife. His aged mother was still living; and it was one of the happiest circumstances connected with his unexpected good fortune, that she had not to remove from the home where she had spent nearly fifty years of her exemplary life.

Mrs. Philip Hurst loved and venerated her husband's mother, and there was no fear that her continued residence in her son's house would ever give rise to the dissensions and jealousies which too frequently attend such a domestic arrangement.

I think I never beheld a more pleasant object than that lady presented, the first time I was admitted into the pretty, bay-windowed room exclusively appropriated to her use, and into which no person entered without special invitation from its mistress. She must have been very lovely in her youth, and still retained traces of beauty in the delicate, transparent complexion and fine unruffled brow, shaded by hair of that silvery whiteness which so agreeably softens the deep lines in an aged face. She had the same bright smile and musically happy laugh as her son; and, like him, was a welcome guest in every cottage in the parish. Dressed always in black silk, and her face shaded by neat close caps of delicate lace, she was to be found, from an early hour in the morning, seated by the old-fashioned casement, busily employed in making articles of clothing for some of her favourites in the village schools. Whenever the weather would permit, her wheeled chair was brought to the door, in which she would make the circuit of the parish, stopping at every house where sickness or sorrow of any kind required her advice or assistance.

Though she was respected and beloved by every one in the place, even by that unfortunate, and sometimes formidable, class called, in a secluded country village, "roughs," she was, to some extent, feared by those who were idle and thriftless.

"Now, Polly Jackson," said she one day, when I had the privilege of walking beside her chair, "what brings you back from the place I procured for you in Reading?"

Polly Jackson, a great, awkward girl of sixteen, stood with one finger in her mouth, gazing at the stern face of the questioner, but without replying to her. Her mother came to the assistance of the delinquent.

"Please, ma'am, she was weak-like and wanted a rest."

"Wanted a rest, indeed! Why don't you tell the truth, and say she wanted a holiday."

"Well, sure," said Polly, encouraged by her mother's support, "and don't a holiday do a body more good than doctor's stuff? I am sure you said so last autumn when you let Nancy Springett go home for a month."

"You are an incorrigible, idle girl. That's what you are Polly! Drive on, Dick!"

This command was issued to the boy who drew the chair.

"Now, my dear," said my venerable friend, as we slowly descended the hill which led to the "town," "I will give you a bit of advice. You may at some future day be mistress of a home in a country-place such as this; if so, never engage a servant who has left her place because she feels 'weak-like.' The martins will not more surely leave the eaves of your house in autumn, than girls like Polly Jackson 'give missus warning,' as soon as they have earned sufficient to lay in a little stock of finery to excite the admiration and envy of their less fortunate companions. That girl remained but six months in the respectable and comfortable situation which, with no little trouble, I succeeded in obtaining for her."

To this lady I confided all my apprehensions

respecting my mother, and, to my great sorrow, she expressed her opinion that nothing but some sudden necessity for exertion would prove effectual to check the progress of the torpor which was gradually stealing over her mental powers.

This anxiety for my mother was speedily removed, but by an event which occasioned the deepest distress to myself.

A letter from Mr. Lancester informed her that Henry had visited his home, and finding it deserted, had gone to him for information respecting his family. "He had," said our informant, "formed some plans for his future career, which he would not explain to him." And he urged my mother to at once hasten to London, and ascertain for herself the extent of her son's wishes, and her own ability and inclination for enabling them to be carried into effect.

My dear mother! how her sweet face brightened as she read of the safety of the beloved prodigal. Now the mists which had settled over her heart cleared away, and the sunshine of hope once more entered it, as she prepared to follow Mr. Lancester's advice to proceed to London, and give her erring son the means of breaking through the toils in which he had been long enmeshed.

It was arranged for Martha to accompany my mother, and that Mrs. Hurst would remain with Esther and myself during their absence.

"God bless you, my dear children!" were her last words before her departure. "I shall soon return to you and bring Henry with me."

How little could she imagine my anguish as I heard the words? For me peace and happiness were over, and again I was the victim of the nervous horrors which had formerly rendered my life a burthen.

For two days we heard nothing from my mother; then there came a letter that was one wail of affliction.

Henry had been ill, was involved in debts and difficulties, from which her duty to her other children would not allow her to extricate him; and unless she did so, he threatened to leave her for ever—to quit the country, and throw himself without friends or resources on a foreign land.

My heart beat with indignation as I read that record of my mother's sufferings. Ought I not to interfere? and, by telling her of Henry's baseness, turn her affection into horror against the murderer of her husband—the midnight spoiler of her own property—the associate of the wretch who had nearly deprived myself of existence!

Esther was unable to account for the restless state of excitement in which I passed those wretched days. Each post brought us letters from my mother or Mr. Lancester; and one of them at last promised to release me from all my terrors. It contained the blessed intelligence that Henry's passage was taken in a vessel bound for Canada: furnished by my mother with ample funds, and, through the interest of Mr. Lancester, with letters of introduction to those in the colony who could aid him in his wish to become a settler there, he was to start, with every advantage the love and care of a mother could provide, in the new race he was to run.

One thing occasioned great pain to my mother—he would leave England without bidding farewell to his brothers and sisters. "The time was too short," he said, "to allow him to do so, as every moment was occupied in preparations for his departure."

Hope and dread struggled together in my heart as I read this letter. Henry away from England! No more doubts and fears respecting him; no longer to live in apprehension of his suddenly appearing among us; of seeing my mother languishing in sorrow on his account; to have the knowledge that the dark curtain had vanished from our home, and that tranquillity and hope might dwell unchecked within it, was such a new state of existence, that no wonder I could not believe in its reality! And that all these mercies would be mine without the painful necessity of meeting my brother, added to my joy and gratitude, for how could I have done so, without shrinking with horror from his Judas-like caresses, and thus wound the heart of his mother by showing my abhorrence of her beloved son?

I never experienced more anxiety than I did at this period of my life. Although each day brought letters detailing the preparations made for his departure, I could not believe but that something would occur to prevent it; that at the eleventh hour some obstacle would interpose, or that he himself would refuse to quit the country.

At length came the joyful news that the day—nay, the very hour—was fixed on which my mother was to bid him farewell on board the vessel, in which he was to cross the Atlantic. It was to be in the afternoon of the twelfth of August. It was the eighth on which I received this letter; four days more, and hope would be changed into blessed certainty! With feverish eagerness, I counted the hours as they dragged heavily away; and when the clock struck the one on which he was to embark, the excitement of the last few weeks reached its climax, and, with an hysterical scream, I fell lifeless on the floor!

CHAPTER IX.

For several days after my mother's return, I was too ill to learn the particulars respecting Henry's departure. When well enough to listen, she told me, unasked, all I required to know. He had sailed at the appointed time, in good health and high spirits, confident of success in his new career, and apparently grateful to her who had supplied all his wants with a bountiful hand.

"We shall hear from him soon," added my mother, when she had spoken of the farewell on board the vessel. "God grant he may prosper in the path he has chosen! But, oh! Nelly, it was with a bitter pang that I parted with my first-born, most probably for ever."

She wept as she uttered the words, and I felt a guilty thrill in my heart at the consciousness that she would shrink from me in horror, could she know the joy with which it was filled by the event which occasioned such anguish to herself.

We were now in daily expectation of a visit from Mr. Lancester, accompanied by his son, and I hoped their society would prove beneficial to my mother's spirits. Some of the old jealousy of my nature was beginning to appear, and I often thought harshly of her, when day after day passed, and she still mourned as one who would not be comforted, at the absence of my unworthy brother. Sometimes I resolved savagely to acquaint her with the proofs of his iniquity I had hitherto sedulously kept from her knowledge. Thank God! I never committed that wicked act.

At the time I was fiercely wrestling with my evil nature, our friends arrived, and by their presence dispelled the gloom which rested over our home.

Gerald Lancester was the only son of our

friend, and we had known and loved him from infancy. He was a few years older than Henry, and shortly after he had attained his one-and-twentieth year, passed the necessary examinations to enable him to practice as a surgeon, and shortly after obtained the appointment of assistant-surgeon in a regiment on the eve of departing for India, where he had remained for the last six years: he had just arrived in England on sick leave.

Gerald had not much altered during his absence; he was more manly in appearance, and his once fair complexion was bronzed by the tropical sun he had been so long under, but his voice was as sweet, and his laugh as frank and merry, as when the night before his departure he had, at our urgent request, exhibited himself in his new uniform, and received — half-laughing, half-ashamed — the compliments I liberally bestowed on his splendid appearance.

He now pretended not to recognise me, but declared the Nelly Travers he had known was a little fat girl, with a turned-up nose and red hair, and that six years could not have transformed her into a tall, slight young lady, with ringlets the colour of a chesnut, and a nose humble enough to bend towards her mouth, instead of endeavouring to reach her eyes.

Gerald had left England just before Esther's dreadful accident, and therefore thought of her only as a lovely, graceful girl, full of health and animation. She was indeed still lovely, but it was beauty of such a fragile and touching nature, that it brought tears into the eyes of those who gazed on it for the first time.

"Is she not sadly altered?" asked my mother, as she followed Gerald from the room after his first interview with the poor girl.

"She was always beautiful," answered he, with emotion, "but I could never have imagined loveliness so exquisite as that she now possesses. It is terrible to think of such a creature, destined to live without even the hope that means may be devised for her relief; surely—surely, Mrs. Travers—some method should be adopted for her recovery!"

"They would be all in vain," said my mother, sadly. "The eminent surgeons who constantly attended her for many months after the accident, assured us that any remedies which might be used would have the effect of causing the return of the frightful spasmodic cramps from which she long suffered. They said it was better she should remain tranquil and free from pain, than be agitated by hopes that could never be realized, and tortured by experiments which could result only in failures."

The arrival of our friends rendered our home more cheerful than it had been since my father's death. The receipt of a few lines from Henry, written in a cheerful and hopeful spirit, shortly after his arrival at Montreal, had removed, at least for a time, my mother's uneasiness respecting his welfare; while Esther, interested and amused by the spirited details of Indian life and society which Gerald related, was heard to laugh as merrily as she did when she beheld him, the night before he left England, patiently stand, at my command, that I might admire the glories of his regimental costume.

As for my own feelings at this time, I used to wonder at them, and accuse myself of insensibility for being so happy, when I had so many painful subjects for reflection. My mother's feeble health — Esther's hopeless condition—the recollection of Henry's wicked conduct—were all things to sadden my present tranquillity; yet I could not help feeling as if misfortune had abandoned us, and peace and joy become permanent inhabitants of our dwelling. And I was right in thinking some blessing was about to be bestowed—one of the greatest which God could vouchsafe me. Gerald had confided to me, as a surgeon, his belief that Esther might, if proper means were employed, rise from the bed, where, for six years, she had lain without hope, and take her place again amongst us. I was utterly incredulous when he first expressed this opinion.

"I do not pledge myself, Nelly," answered he, in reply to my doubts, "that Esther will ever perfectly recover, but from all I have gleaned from Martha, I am convinced her spine has not received the serious injury Mr. L—— imagined, and that under a different mode of treatment she will ultimately be restored to some degree of health. I only wonder she has survived such long confinement to one room; but she must eventually sink under such a regimen. The first steps taken must be to improve the tone of her general health, and the best tonics to be administered are hope and fresh air. If allowed to try the effects of these stimulants on her system for some little time, I would boldly adopt other measures. Do try, Nelly, if you can gain your mother's permission for me to so far exert my medical skill. Why should she not be moved daily from her own room to the one adjoining it, which appears only used as a receptacle for lumber? Trifling as such a change may seem to you, it would be of incalculable benefit to that poor imprisoned girl. Use your influence with your mother to effect this first step towards our object."

"I fear," answered I, "that Esther herself will raise more objections to your plan than my mother. She entertains such fearful recollections of the agony she suffered when under medical treatment, that she has always said she was contented to remain in her present crippled state, if she could be free from their repetition."

"She need know nothing of our plans, Nelly," persisted the young surgeon. "Only let your mother give us her sanction, and do not fear for the result."

With a great deal of persuasion my mother was induced to give her permission for Gerald to try his experiment. And as soon as it was obtained we all set heartily to work to transform the lumber-room into a pretty boudoir.

It was part of Gerald's plan that Esther should be kept in ignorance of his intentions. She was not to be agitated with either hopes or fears till the first step was gained—her being safely conveyed into the adjoining room.

It was a labour of love to all of us to get it prettily arranged. Mrs. Hurst chose the carpet, and had it fitted, Martha and I made the curtains, and Gerald hung the pretty, bright-patterned paper, he had chosen for the walls, while Mr. Hurst brought from the Vicarage some of his most treasured volumes, to scatter on sofa and tables, and his mother lent some rare and beautiful china to ornament the mantelpiece and brackets.

I think we all felt delighted when, our labours completed, we looked round the pretty, cheerful room, we had so industriously worked at. The morning following its completion, the experiment, at once longed for and dreaded, was to be made. Mrs. Hurst had promised to be with us when the moment arrived, and we were all assembled in Esther's room at the hour it was customary for Martha to place her on her couch by the window.

"I don't know the reason, good people," cried she, cheerfully, as we stood round her bed, "why you come into the room before the usual hour of my receptions; but something extraordinary appears, as the country people say, 'to be up.' Pray admire the pink ribbons with which my cap and gown are decorated, and then, if Martha is quite ready, I shall be glad if she will carry me to the window."

Martha looked nervously at my mother, who, pale as Esther, stood at the foot of the bed. I saw that what was to be done must be done promptly, and said, "Yes, be quick, Martha; and, Esther, as Gerald has a little surprise for you under the window, I shall not allow you to catch a glimpse of it till you are on the sofa."

As I spoke, I enveloped her head in a light shawl, and the next moment she was in Martha's arms, who carried her light burthen so quickly, that she was unconscious of the change till the covering was removed from her face. For a moment we were frightened by the wild look of astonishment that passed over it, as she gazed at the novel scene, as if in doubt of its reality.

The cheerful voice of Mrs. Hurst was the first to break the silence. "My dear Esther, welcome to your fairy palace; and here comes the magician you must thank for it."

Gerald, who was watching from the door the effects of his scheme, now advanced to Esther, and taking her hand, begged her to pardon him, if her removal had distressed or alarmed her.

"God bless you!" she answered, "for all your kindness to the poor crippled girl, and believe how grateful she is for this proof of your anxiety to afford her pleasure. Why, I shall dream to-night that I am well again, and able to take my place amongst you as formerly; and then," she added, with a deep sigh, "awake to find myself helpless and dependent as ever."

Gerald's voice faltered as he replied, "Esther, remember the words of Him who gave sight to the blind, and feet to the lame, 'All things are possible to him that believes.'"

CHAPTER X.

From the day Esther was allowed to hope, a marked improvement became visible in her health; before the expiration of a fortnight she was carried down stairs, and placed in a curious, but comfortable, wheeled couch, which Gerald had had constructed under his own personal superintendence by the village carpenter.

With this new stimulus for the energies of my mother, her own health and spirits seemed rapidly to improve.

Esther appeared now the one object in which her hopes were centered; and, from regarding Gerald with feelings almost of dislike, as an impudent pretender to medical science, she went to the other extreme, and considered him endowed with almost superhuman skill.

Certainly my sister's marked improvement gave us every confidence in his assurances of complete ultimate recovery. Every day the weather would permit, she spent some hours in the open air; and, thanks to Gerald's admirable contrivance, she had made acquaintance with every part of the village of Brookfields. At first she had a great objection to being gazed at by those she encountered, but this feeling soon wore off, and she took pleasure in conversing with the children who lingered in the road when they saw the sick lady's "funny" carriage approaching. She speedily, too, became a great friend and ally of the elder Mrs. Hurst; and side by side did the wheeled chair of the aged and the couch of the youthful invalid perambulate the shady lanes and quiet roads of the pretty village.

"I have a favour to ask of you," said Mrs. Philip Hurst, one day in October, to my mother. "To-morrow is the eighty-second birthday of my husband's mother, and we wish you to honour it by spending it at the Vicarage. Gerald tells me the exertion will do Esther no harm; and I have a room ready for Martha and her for the night, as he thinks it would be imprudent for her to be out after sunset. Now, don't decline—which I see you are about to do—till I have spoken to Esther. Would you like it, my dear?"

"Very much," replied my sister, frankly.

"Then I will not accept mamma's denial. We shall expect you to luncheon, and after that you must be wheeled into the church, and inspect the monuments you have often expressed a wish to see."

It was a great treat for me at all times to spend a day at the Vicarage; but to be accompanied there by Esther, was a delight I had never anticipated. To show her all the wonders of Mr. Hurst's study; to open, as I knew he would allow me, the drawers of his cabinet, and exhibit the collection of minerals he valued so highly; above all, to see her reclining by the side of his venerable mother, listening to the stories of past times, which gave such pleasure to myself, was an amount of happiness I could hardly bring myself to believe in.

The early years of the elder Mrs. Hurst had been passed in the "great city," where her father had for a long period held a curacy. From infancy she had been familiar with stories connected with his ministry; and these she related with such graphic fidelity, that I, for a time was "transported beyond this ignorant present," and lived amidst the scenes invoked by the memory of my aged friend.

I felt sure Esther would delight in these old-world stories as much as I did. What past events should I ask to have conjured up for the benefit of my sister? She was not, like me, fascinated by tales of gloom and horror. She would feel no pleasure in hearing of Lord Ferrers proceeding to his execution in a coach and six, dressed in his wedding suit of white and silver; for the reason, as he stated, that if he had never been married he should never have been hanged; of the levity he displayed throughout the slow progress of that fearful journey, impeded as it was by the enormous crowd who flocked to witness the execution of a "lord"; and of the stern rebuke administered to him by the chaplain who attended him.

Neither would she care to hear of the fearful scenes witnessed, when a child, by the venerable narrator, when London was in the hands of a ferocious mob, which, under the plea of religious excitement, committed frightful atrocities on the lives and property of the peaceful citizens.

No; she would shrink with terror from scenes like these. But she would like to hear of the day when the "Good King," in state procession, but humility of heart, went to St. Paul's for the purpose of thanking Almighty God for his restoration to reason. Of the crowds which thronged the streets through which he passed; and of the deep, heartfelt "God bless your Majesty," uttered as by one voice, by the countless thousands who that day, with tears of joy, hailed their beloved sovereign.

It was not that I was ignorant of many of the events I heard from Mrs. Hurst. I had read of them as historical facts, but it was with very different feelings I listened to their recital from the lips of one who had either witnessed them herself or lived from childhood with those who had been actors in the scenes; and I did not doubt Esther would hear them with the same interest as myself.

I knew that our present happy life must soon be over, that Mr. Lancester and Gerald would leave us in a few days; and then I feared — all anxiety for Esther past — my mother would become the victim of gloomy doubts and apprehensions on account of the long silence of Henry. Only once had we heard from him since he left England; and in the eagerness my mother expressed each morning for the arrival of the letter-bag, I beheld, with certainty, the return of her uneasiness for her son.

But these things should not be thought of on the morrow. Esther's first visit should be marked with a white stone, and no dread of the future should stain its purity.

We went to the Vicarage at the appointed time, and happily the day passed away.

Esther, perhaps, had the greatest amount of pleasure, for to her all had the charm of novelty. In the afternoon she was taken into the church. That old building was a noted place for tourists, and very seldom during the summer did a day elapse without bringing strangers to inspect it. On that account Esther had never before entered it; as she was morbidly sensitive respecting being gazed at as she lay helpless on her mattress. That day, fortunately, proved an exception to the rule, and my dear sister was not annoyed by the inquisitive gaze of holiday sight-seers.

The church well deserved its reputation, although but a fragment of the original edifice. It must at one time not only have been of great extent, but of considerable importance, for it had been chosen as the final resting-place of many of the Knight Templars, whose effigies still remained in the aisle and chancel, blocking up, with their large raised tombs, the small portion of the church which was preserved for public worship.

The exterior of the building was covered with ivy; from the very summit of the square tower to the ground there was barely an inch of gray stone to be discerned; and to this beautiful natural protection was to be attributed the preservation of so much of the building as remained.

"I have often been surprised," said Mr. Lancester, as Mr. Hurst was industriously pointing out to him the evidences of its former size, "that such large churches are frequently met with in secluded districts such as this. The parish has never, that I can learn, been more populated than at present; and yet when this building was erected it must have been capable of containing ten times the number of those who could have resided within an attainable distance."

"The piety of our ancestors," replied the Vicar, "if not more sincere, was at least more costly than our own. They appear to have considered more the Majesty of Him to whom their buildings were dedicated, than the number of the worshippers who would assemble within the walls."

In the evening we all assembled for tea in the elder Mrs. Hurst's pretty sitting-room; who insisted, on that occasion, on doing the honours of the table. Esther was placed on a sofa by the bright fire, and Gerald, seated by her side, was anxiously inquiring whether she felt much fatigued.

"Oh, no!" she answered, in a low voice, "it has been a day of unmixed pleasure! How shall I ever be able to thank you, as I ought, for the blessings you have, under God, been the means of conferring on me? When I think of the hours I have passed this day, and contrast them with those which for six long years dragged wearily and hopelessly away, I feel as if I must be the most insensible of human beings not to be able better to express the gratitude which fills my heart!"

"Hush, Esther!" was the whispered reply. "Do not thank me for conferring such great happiness on myself. To see you restored to health, is one of the two earthly blessings I pray God to grant me!"

At this moment the cheerful voice of Mrs. Philip Hurst was heard—

"Come, young people, you are all much too quiet! I think we had better push the table up to Esther's corner, and have a round game to make us merry."

"Is card-playing allowed at the Vicarage?" asked Mr. Lancester.

"My dear sir, anything is allowed at the Vicarage that is allowed in other sober, orderly places. Why not? Philip does not love his duty less for liking a game of whist, chess, or backgammon! I believe some very far-sighted people can perceive a distinction between playing with bits of painted wood and painted paper, and will spend hours over a chess-board, though they groan at the mention of cards. I must own my eyes are not so keen!"

"But, Mrs. Hurst," said I, "if Mr. Lancester has any prejudices regarding playing cards in a vicarage, pray let us respect them. Mr. Hurst promised to light up the cosmorama to-night, and I am sure we shall all prefer it either to loo or *vingt-et-une*. Besides,

I am impatient to behold Mr. Hamlyn's famous picture."

Now this cosmorama was the one hobby of the good Vicar. His favourite amusement was painting in oil colours; and, as his pictures were small, he had constructed a vehicle in which to exhibit to the best advantage the fruits of his industry. I did not in the least understand how it was managed, but, by looking through glasses, which resembled the bulls'-eyes of a lantern, the pictures were magnified to an astonishing degree.

He delighted most in depicting naval engagements, which I thought rather curious subjects for the pencil of a man of peace; but he justified his choice by saying they were more effective than any other when viewed through the bulls'-eyes. These magnifiers were placed in a very elegant-looking piece of cabinet work, which I, at first sight, mistook for the model of a sedan chair. I had been frequently favoured by a sight of the battles of the Nile and Copenhagen, the death of Nelson, and the other celebrated engagements which it was the delight of the reverend artist to portray; but there was one picture, the pride of his collection, which he had frequently promised to show me as soon as it was returned from London, where it had been sent to have some accidental injury repaired. It was the work of an artist-friend of Mr. Hurst, painted expressly for the cosmorama some years previously, when Mr. Hamlyn was a guest at the Vicarage; and as it had, I knew, arrived from town the previous day, I claimed the fulfilment of the promise I had received.

When the lights were properly arranged in the cosmorama, Mr. Hurst invited me to have the first view of the restored picture.

The subject was Jezebel instructing Ahab how to obtain the vineyard of Naboth the Jezreelite.

Ahab was reclining on a couch, and his wicked queen, standing by his side, was pouring into his willing ears the scheme by which he might seize the inheritance of his poor subject.

I was no judge of art; but, as I looked at

this picture, I felt it was by a very different artist to the one who had composed the famous sea-fights with which I was so well acquainted.

The first glance fascinated my attention. The figure of the cruel queen of Israel was the object which immediately rivetted the eye of the spectator.

Gorgeously attired in Eastern costume, she bent gracefully over the bed of her weak and wicked husband. Her hand was raised in an attitude to excite his attention to her words, while her face beamed with an expression of triumphant and malicious satisfaction, as if she already exulted in the success of her perfidious stratagem. The face was beautiful, the features perfect in their regularity, but of a decided Eastern type of character. It was wonderful that any art of the painter could have thrown into a countenance so lovely such an expression of ruthless cruelty as was portrayed in hers.

As I continued to gaze, unable to remove my eyes from the face at once so attractive and repelling, I felt a shudder of horror creep over my frame. The beautiful Jezebel resembled exactly, both in feature and expression, the woman whom I had beheld that fatal night with her arm round the neck of my brother. Just that look of fierce malignity did her face wear, as, snatching the knife from the table, she appealed to his remembrance of the manner in which he had known her use a similar weapon. Pale and trembling, I drew back from the cosmorama.

"Well, is it not good?" asked Mr. Hurst, eagerly; "but you have not half looked at it. Just observe the beauty of that young Jezebel; well might poor Hamlyn wish to paint her in such a character, for she was cut out by nature to play a similar part. She took great delight in sitting for that picture, and when Hamlyn regretted she looked too youthful fully to realize the idea, the young vixen—she was only seventeen at the time—laughed, and said, 'Look at me now,' and she actually did contrive, by throwing that abominably wicked expression into her face, to make herself look half-a-dozen years older than she was."

"Whose portrait is it?" asked Gerald, who had been looking at it in evident admiration. "I should say it was not a face likely to belong to any village beauty."

"But it really is so," replied Mr. Hurst. "Have you never noticed the tall, melancholy-looking woman, who lives with her father at Sandhill Farm? This Jezebel is her only child; and when the death of her husband, only two years after her marriage, left her without a home, old Wishart gladly received his daughter and grandchild at the farm."

"But is that girl in the village now?" asked Gerald, with his eyes still fixed on the painting; "surely I must have noticed such a face had I ever beheld it."

"There is a sad tale connected with Hannah Locksley," said Mr. Hurst; "she left Brookfields some years ago, shortly, indeed, after Hamlyn painted that portrait, and her mother has never been seen to smile since the day she quitted it."

I breathed more freely when I heard who was the original of the picture which had awakened such painful recollections. Trusting my imagination had magnified the resemblance to the woman I had such reason to remember with dread, I again looked at it, and this time persuaded myself I had been deceived. Still, I was too much agitated by the thoughts to which its sight had given rise to shake off the depression I felt, and had to plead severe headache to account for my silence during the remainder of the evening.

Esther and Gerald bestowed the proper amount of admiration on the naval engagements, and did not appear to feel any horror at the expression of wickedness on the face of the beautiful Jezebel, which, to my eyes, transformed the loveliness of an angel into that of an evil spirit; but they had not seen the terrible woman of whom it reminded me and could admire without shuddering as they gazed.

With my mind filled with painful memories, I accompanied my mother home, and thus the day, of which I had resolved no clouds should darken the brightness, closed over me in gloom.

I arose the next morning with brighter thoughts. Why should I be wretched because I had seen a face which reminded me of one I would willingly forget I had ever beheld? Henry was beyond the reach of her fatal influence, and it was not probable she would ever again cross my path.

I did not require to witness the emotion which both patient and surgeon evinced at parting, to assure me of the feelings which had sprung up in the heart of each. I knew well at the time I overheard their whispered conversation in Mrs. Hurst's room, the meaning of Gerald's words, that Esther's recovery was one of the two boons he hoped God would vouchsafe him—the other, I felt sure, was dependent on the first being granted.

When our friends left us, it was arranged that I should write to Gerald weekly, and acquaint him with all the particulars connected with Esther, and he promised us a visit fortnightly, in order that he might himself judge of the progress she was making towards recovery.

At his third visit he requested her to try if she could stand, supported by his arm. To our great delight, she did so, without pain or difficulty.

"Now, Esther," cried Gerald, triumphantly, "I have the happiness of telling you that all doubt is at an end. In six months I trust you will be able to walk without support."

My mother burst into tears when these blessed words were spoken, but Esther for a moment looked as though she did not comprehend the full meaning of what she heard, and then covered her face with her hands, as if a vision too bright and dazzling to be gazed at was before her. Half frightened at her silence, I was about to speak to her, when, in a broken, trembling voice, she murmured,

"What return can I make unto the Lord for all the mercies he has vouchsafed towards me? May He grant that the remembrance of them may be for ever before me, and that I may always say from my heart, 'It is good for me that I have been afflicted!'"

CHAPTER XI.

As autumn deepened into winter, my spirits became, to some extent, saddened by the dreariness of all around me. Deep fogs rested for days together over the hills, and shrouded every tree and hedge in their misty gloom. Gerald had long forbidden Esther to venture out, and my mother could never be prevailed on to accompany me in the walks she insisted on my taking daily.

Since the night I had seen the portrait of Hannah Locksley, I had taken a strange pleasure in visiting Sandhill Farm, and conversing with her mother. She was a woman of far superior manners than it is usual to meet with in her rank of life. There was a mournful quietude about her, which gave a species of refinement both to her speech and actions. I never saw a smile gleam across her face; its expression was that of pious, humble resignation, to an evil which seemed ever present to her heart.

Her father was a man approaching eighty years of age, and as restless and impatient as his daughter was quiet and resigned. He appeared to have but one ruling passion—the love of money—and I soon discovered I was no welcome visitant at the farm unless I administered to this foible.

Mrs. Locksley herself always seemed glad when she saw me enter. I could not tell why the idea occurred to me, but I fancied I, in some way, reminded her of her lost daughter. Often she would regard me till her eyes filled with tears, and once I heard her mutter as she gazed, "So like, and yet so different."

"Who am I like?" inquired I, impulsively.

"One that it would be sin to name before you, young lady;" and the poor mother, overcome by the harshness of her own words, threw her apron over her head, and wept aloud.

Inexpressibly shocked, I stood irresolute whether to depart, or remain and try to soothe the grief my words had called forth.

Presently removing the covering from her face, she advanced towards me and taking my hands, said, "Pray to God that He may save you from temptation, and though it can never assail you in the form it did my wretched child, yet pray that misconduct of yours may never draw bitter tears from your mother's eyes. But I need not fear it; there is that in your face which tells me you will ever be good and true to your duties." She kissed me tenderly on the forehead, and the next instant the words, "Oh! God, how like, and yet how unlike!" broke again from her lips.

At this moment the old man entered the kitchen. He looked angrily at his weeping daughter, and then said, gruffly, "What's this to-do about? What does the young madam want, Hannah? I s'pose she does want summut; she wouldn't come taking up folk's time for nought."

I saw the flush of mingled shame and sorrow that passed over his daughter's cheek at his rudeness, and hastened to answer the old man.

"To be sure I want something, Master Wishart—I want some of your chickens, and hope you will go with me to the meadow and choose them for me."

The angry look left the farmer's cheek at the prospect of gain, and taking his stick from the corner in which he had placed it when he entered, he said, "Come along, then, and I'll show you the best chickens in the parish; but they are very dear," added he, with a cunning look; "chickens is money now, I tell you."

I suffered him to place his own price on those I selected, and in high good humour he returned with me to the house, where I pulled out my purse to pay for my purchases.

As I did so, Mrs. Locksley, who had recovered from the state of agitation in which I left her, and was busily engaged in preparing the dinner, said, "How much a couple did you charge the young lady for the chickens, father?"

"Mind thy own business, Hannah," was

the answer, "and leave me to mind mine. The chickens are four shillings a couple, and cheap at the money."

I had placed a sovereign on the table, and before her father could clutch it, Mrs Locksley took it up, and putting it in a little canvass bag she drew from her pocket, gave me from the same receptacle fifteen shillings.

"The chickens are half-a-crown a couple, Miss Ellen; father has made a mistake. I will send them up to 'Oakdens' in the course of the afternoon;" and before the old man's wrath had time to explode I had left the house, in compliance with an entreating look from the poor daughter.

From that time I became a great favourite with Master Wishart. He always appeared to think he had cheated me out of the disputed eighteenpence a couple in the chickens, and looked at me whenever I entered the house, with a sort of chuckling complacency, as if exulting in his own powers of extortion.

Gradually I became acquainted with the history of Hannah Locksley, as far as it was known in her native village.

A quick, clever child, of remarkable beauty, she was the idol of her grandfather, who from her infancy petted and fostered her every caprice. In vain did her mother endeavour to check the ungovernable temper of her child. The old man would not suffer his darling to be thwarted, and openly encouraged her to rebel against her mother's authority. In consequence of her positive refusal to attend the village school, she reached the age of thirteen without instruction of any kind. To the surprise of all that knew her, she then signified her wish of being placed at a boarding-school in a neighbouring town, where she remained three years.

Hannah possessed abilities as well as beauty, and the vanity which caused her to be ashamed of her ignorance, when old enough to comprehend the disadvantage it might prove to her in after life, was sufficiently powerful to enable her to bear the restraint under which those three years were passed.

She appeared to have made good use of the time she remained in the polite seminary of the Misses Snatchell, where she frequently bore off the prizes from those who had ridiculed her ignorance when she first appeared amongst them, and her superiority over her companions induced her so greatly to over-rate her own acquirements, that she applied, shortly after her leaving school, for the situation of governess in the family of a lady of rank in the vicinity. To her surprise and indignation, she was politely informed she was not qualified for the office.

This was a great blow to the proud, vain girl, and from that time she abandoned all thoughts of procuring a situation, and ruled henceforth more absolutely than ever over her doting grandfather, who denied her no indulgence he had the means of gratifying.

Shortly after Mr. Hamlyn had taken her portrait as Jezebel, she received an invitation from a former schoolfellow to spend a few days with her at W——, during the race-week. A day previous to the one fixed for her return, her grandfather received a letter from her, announcing her intention of remaining from home some time longer, and desiring money might be sent her for the purpose of providing her with a new dress, for a ball to which she was to accompany her friend.

The farmer had never refused a request made to him by his darling, even when it was for some of his hoarded wealth; penurious to all others, he was lavishly profuse to her, and more than she had demanded was sent to her.

At the ball, for which Hannah required this dress, her beauty excited universal admiration. But one person in particular, a stranger who had attended the races, and who was described as a man of a bold, but handsome, appearance, devoted himself to her during the evening.

Several days elapsed beyond the one specified for her return, and still Hannah had some excuse for delay; more gaieties were in prospect, and more money requisite for the finery she required to attend them.

Wherever she went at that time, she was accompanied by the man whose acquaintance she had made at the ball; and Mrs. Locksley, hearing of this from a neighbour who had met them together in the streets of W——, became so seriously uneasy at her protracted absence, that she resolved herself to go and ascertain the reason she did not return.

The day before she was to do so, Hannah arrived at the farm more beautiful and arrogant than ever, and refused, contemptuously, to answer the questions of her anxious mother relative to the stranger with whom she had become so intimately acquainted during her absence.

However great the admiration felt by that person for Hannah Locksley, it was not strong enough to induce him to follow her to Brookfields; but that did not appear in the least to annoy the object of it. Her mother quickly guessed she was carrying on a correspondence with him, for she frequently found her writing in her own room, and knew she received letters in a writing with which she herself was unacquainted.

Six weeks after her return from W——, her grandfather attended a large cattle fair some miles distant, to which he had sent a considerable quantity of stock. He returned late at night, highly delighted with his day's work, and drawing a heavy canvass bag from his pocket, emptied its contents on the table, and then told Hannah to take from them as much as would buy her the prettiest gown in W——.

"Then I'll take this note, grandfather!" replied she, taking one for the value of twenty pounds, from the glistening heap of gold amongst which it lay.

The old farmer looked a little astonished at the amount it took for such a purpose, and laughing, good-humouredly, said—

"Well, lass, it is a good thing for you I did not wait till the morning to give you a gown! If I had, I reckon you would have had less to have bought it with! But I can afford it—the stock sold well—and I got paid for it all in hard cash. I would none of folks' cheques I knew naught about. No, no; I am a little too deep to be done at this time of day. But now, lock up all that money in the big chest in my room, girl; and to-morrow I'll give you a treat to W—— to spend your note."

The next morning Mrs. Locksley and her father waited breakfast in vain for Hannah. She was gone, and with her the weighty money-bag entrusted to her to lock in the chest the previous night!

From that night her history was a blank to the inhabitants of Brookfields.

One fine afternoon, early in December, I walked to the Vicarage to inquire after Mrs. Hurst, who had been unwell for some days. When I proposed to leave, she pressed me to remain till her son returned home.

"He will go back with you, Nelly; and Jane and I will be good-natured, and spare him to remain to tea with you."

Glad to return with such an ally against melancholy as Mr. Hurst, I gladly consented to await his return; but when seven o'clock struck, and he was still absent, I resolved to leave without him. It had long been dark, but the moon was rising, and I had no fear of walking alone through the lanes which I must traverse as the nearest way to my home; and I, therefore, positively refused to allow one of Mr. Hurst's servants to accompany me.

I had passed the turning which led to Sandhill Farm, when I became aware that I was followed by some person. The hedges on each side of the lane nearly obscured the light of the moon, but, as I stopped and turned my head, I could discern the figure of a woman a few yards distant.

Relieved by finding it was one of my own sex, and coming at once to the conclusion that Mrs. Hurst had sent one of the servants after me, I called out, "Is that you, Fanny?"

It was not Fanny's voice which answered me; it was not Fanny's hand which the next instant rested on my arm.

"No, Miss Nelly, that is not my name. It is almost too dark for you to see my face, but I have no doubt you remember the pleasant circumstances attending our first meeting."

The voice was that of the woman I had seen that dreadful night, and the shudder which passed over my frame whenever I even thought of her, now shook me convulsively as I endeavoured to free my arm from her hold.

"Let me go," said I, in a voice so low, I hardly heard the words I uttered. "For God's sake, let me go!"

"Do you suppose," said the wretch, in a mocking tone, "that I am fool enough to let you go before I have told you my errand, after I have come so far in search of you, too! Now listen! I want money and you must give it me. I will be at the bottom of your orchard to-night at ten o'clock. You perceive, stranger as I am in the place, I know the locality of your home. Be there with fifty pounds, or you will bitterly repent not doing so!"

I listened in amazement to this vile woman's audacity, and then indignation mastering the dread I had at first felt, I exclaimed, "Give you money—meet you to-night! How dare you thus address me? Are you not afraid I shall have you apprehended for the robbery you committed in my mother's house? Thank God I have no cause to fear you now!"

"So that is your cue—is it?" said my companion. "You think your brother is so far away that you can afford to be saucy—do you? Now, mark my words: If you do not act as I have commanded—mind, commanded is the word I use!—I will take care that the dainty mother you cherish with such tenderness, shall know that of her eldest son which will stab her to the heart! I don't think she will feel particularly happy when informed of the true history of her silver dishes and tankards! Now you may go—I have done with you till ten o'clock. If you do not then obey me, I will find my way into your mother's room in the dead of night, and tell her that of her son which will make her regret the hour she gave him birth!"

Roused, by these threats, to exertion, I answered, "My brother is beyond your reach, you cannot harm him. You may acquaint my mother with the particulars connected with the dreadful night I first beheld you—and, as you say, it will wound her mother's heart—but, thank God! you cannot injure him, or even his reputation; for you cannot assail it without rendering yourself and the man who so nearly murdered me, liable to punishment. You dare not, for your own sake, tell the truth respecting the robbery at my mother's house."

"You will see what I can, and what I dare do, Miss Nelly!"

At this instant I heard the sound of Mr. Hurst, whistling. It was his habit to do so when walking alone in the quiet lanes.

The woman's ear detected the sound as soon as my own, and she said—

"Some one is coming, but do not imagine I will not fulfil my threat to the very letter. Fifty pounds by ten o'clock to-night! or......"

And without concluding the sentence, she held up her finger in a menacing attitude, and turning into the lane which led to Sandhill Farm, was out of sight before I was joined by Mr. Hurst.

"Well, Nelly!" he cried, here I am sent to see Jane's pet lamb does not go astray in the dark; and really it does appear as if you required a shepherd, for by this time you ought to be much nearer your fold!"

I was unable to reply to his cheerful greeting. I still trembled violently, and he anxiously inquired whether I had been frightened at being alone so late. "And by the way, Nelly, did I not see some one leave you just before I joined you?"

"Yes," said I, blushing at my equivocation, "a woman was importuning me for money, and I was alarmed at her vehemence."

"Some impudent gipsy tramp, I dare say. Don't tremble so, Nelly—you are safe with me. But I am very glad I came just at the moment I did. I must caution mamma, when we get home, not to allow you to wander about so late in the day."

"Pray do not mention anything of my alarm," said I; "you know how soon my mother is agitated. It is foolish to be so timid, but it will be a warning to me not to be out after dark again."

He readily gave me the promise I requested, and chatted with his usual gaiety the rest of the way home.

When we reached it, I left him in the hall, and hastening at once to my own room, endeavoured to collect my thoughts sufficiently to decide how I ought to act respecting the menaces of that fearful woman. I did not heed her threats regarding Henry, and only wondered at her audacity in venturing on such absurd statements respecting him; but I recognised the power she had of inflicting anguish on my mother, and, to spare her, I must devise some mode of purchasing the woman's silence.

But how was I to do so? I had not five shillings of my own, nor did I know any way by which I could obtain it. Should I tell Mr. Hurst, and be guided by his counsels? No; for besides the pain I should experience in acquainting him with my brother's wickedness, I felt certain he would advise a course of action I should shrink from following— to myself baffle the schemes of that vile creature, by informing my mother of all she could impart.

This I felt would be the advice a friend would give me, but no one but myself could tell the miseries which might arise from putting it in action. I saw, in imagination, Esther again transformed into the helpless, crippled state from which she had just been released, and my mother lying in one of the frightful fits of syncope to which she became liable after my father's death, and which, I was told, would infallibly follow any violent mental emotion. These thoughts decided me.

This terrible adversary must be bribed, but how?

I ran over in my mind the value of the few trinkets I possessed. Was it possible they would be accepted in lieu of the sum demanded? There was the watch given me by my father on that wretched thirteenth birthday, the locket presented at the same time by my young brothers, and a few rings and brooches given to me on similar occasions. These comprised my store of valuables; and even if I reconciled myself to the pain of parting with such memorials of affection I felt sure they were wholly inadequate for the purpose of satisfying the rapacity of my foe.

While in this state of terrible uncertainty, Martha entered my room, and with the quick eye of affection discovered something serious had occurred to distress me. Thankful that I could impart the events of the evening to one whom I knew would not betray them, I told her all that had passed in my interview with the woman in the lane. I did not imagine that my nurse could aid me, but I had before felt the relief of confiding my anxieties to that kind friend.

Poor Martha! I think her misery was as great as my own. I am sure she was equally anxious to preserve my mother and sister from being shocked by the discovery of Henry's guilty participation in the robbery of the plate—but how was it to be prevented?

After a few minutes spent in reflection, she said, "I will tell you what you must do. You must meet this woman at the time she fixed, and promise that she shall have the money in a week."

"But, nurse," said I, in astonishment, "where am I to get it from by that time?"

"I can get it, dear, but I must write to London for it. You know I have money out at use in a bank there."

"Oh! no—no!—Martha," said I, greatly distressed at such a proposal, "I cannot consent to deprive you of the money you have saved for your old age."

"Now, don't talk nonsense, pet. The money is for you and Miss Esther, so what does it matter when you have it. And as for my old age—you won't turn me away when I am unable to work, will you?"

The idea of turning Martha away was such an absurd one, that I could not refrain from smiling.

"That's right, dear, laugh at your old nurse, if you like; and now lie down quietly till the time comes for you to meet this wretch. I wish I could go with you, but it is just the time I go up-stairs with Miss Esther, and we must be careful not to excite any suspicions by acting in an unusual manner. I will tell your mamma you would rather remain quiet, and then you won't be disturbed."

It was not nine when Martha left me, and during the hour of solitude which followed what wretchedness did I suffer! Suppose the delay I must solicit was refused?—that my enemy would insist on the immediate payment of her iniquitous demand, and in default of it should apply to my mother, as she had threatened, for the sum she was unable to procure from myself?

It was with feelings of positive relief that I rose from the bed a few minutes before the appointed time, and prepared to meet my fate. Wrapping round me the large shawl Martha had placed near me for the purpose, I stole softly down the stairs, and opening the shutters of the dining-room she had left unfastened, I stepped into the garden.

The moon was shining brightly as I passed along the path which led to the orchard, but the night was wild and stormy, and occasionally dark, heavy clouds quite obscured its light. When I reached the appointed spot, it was so dark that I was unable to distinguish whether any one was waiting on the opposite side of the low wall which separated the orchard from the meadows beyond it. In a moment, however, I heard a voice say,

"It is well for yourself you are so punctual. Now, give me the money; I have no wish to remain longer here in the cold."

In trembling accents I answered that I had not the money with me, and implored her forbearance for a week, when I promised I would obtain it for her.

A low, mocking laugh was the answer I received to this petition for delay. "Do you hear that, Jasper?" said the woman; and I saw by the light of the moon, from which a large cloud had just rolled, that a man leant against the wall a short distance from the spot where the woman was standing.

I could not distinctly see his face as he approached the place where I stood, but too well did I recognise the name by which he was addressed. It was the man who had given me that murderous blow on the night I had detected him removing the plate from my mother's house.

"What do I say to that?" said the ruffian, in a light, jesting tone. "Why, I say that if she does not give us 'meal we'll have malt' —if she does not give us money we'll have revenge. We should prefer being agreeable and pleasant to a lady, and take the money, but if she would sooner go and see her brother in prison in a few days, and save her tin, let her."

I took a desperate resolution when the man uttered the last words—I would brave them —anything at that moment appeared preferable to being exposed to such scenes as this; I forgot all but *self*, and answered, "Do as you please, I have not the money. If you choose to wait for it till the time I have named, I will procure it for you; if not, I will acquaint my friends this night with all that you can reveal likely to grieve my mother —for whose sake alone I have consented to be here now—and they will act towards you as they think best."

Both man and woman were evidently startled at my words. They whispered together for a short time, and then the latter said, " Will you promise faithfully to bring the fifty pounds here, and at this hour next week, and to bring it *alone ?*"

" Yes; on condition that you do not molest me or mine in the interval, and that you likewise promise never to trouble me again."

" We will leave promises for the future, till I see how you keep yours of the present, Miss Nelly. Come, Jasper."

"Stay a moment, Rachel," said the man. "I want to express my admiration of the admirable manner in which our young friend has behaved to-night. It makes me feel more regret than ever that I was compelled by the laws of self-preservation to give her such an unpleasant tap on the head the night of our first meeting. I am sure she will accept this apology, and kiss and be friends."

While speaking, the wretch vaulted over the low wall, and placed his arm round my waist. With a loud scream I burst from his grasp, and rushed frantically towards the house. I could hear him pursue me for some paces, and then suddenly stop at the voice of his companion. I never paused till I had entered the window by which I had left the house, and then, in the same hurried manner, closed and barred the shutters. In my agitation I had not observed that a light was burning in the room, but as with a deep sigh of relief I sunk in a seat near the window, I perceived that Mr. Hurst was gazing at me with a look of amazement.

"Good God! Nelly," cried he, "where have you been at such an hour, and what has alarmed you?"

"I have only been to the bottom of the garden," stammered I, in the greatest confusion, "and I was frightened by hearing footsteps behind me as I returned."

"But surely, Nelly, you will tell me the reason you left the house at such a time?"

At this moment, to my great relief, Martha entered the room. She looked astonished at beholding me with Mr. Hurst, and anxiously inquired what was the matter.

"The matter is this, nurse," said Mr. Hurst; "I was searching for a book I wished to take home with me, when Miss Ellen rushed in at the window, and closed and barred the shutters in such trembling haste, as showed she was fearful of pursuit; I am, therefore, using the privilege of a friend, and inquiring how she came to leave the house at such an hour."

"I can tell you, sir," said Martha, promptly. "Miss Nelly has not felt right all the evening, and we both thought a walk in the garden would do more to relieve her than anything else. The moon was shining very bright when she went out, and I was going to her the moment Miss Esther was in bed."

Mr. Hurst's look of painful surprise vanished at Martha's words, and he answered in his usual cheerful voice, "You see, nurse, it won't do for young ladies to ramble by moonlight, even in such a quiet place as this. You must find some other remedy for her headaches in future."

When once more in my own room, I related to Martha all that had occurred, and the bitter tears of humiliation and shame rolled down my cheeks as I told of the insult I had received. This part of my narrative affected Martha greatly.

"You must not meet these people alone again, my dear child," said she, when I had finished. "I will take them the money this night week, and then, I pray God, we may see no more of them."

CHAPTER XII.

It was on a Wednesday evening I went through the painful scenes I have detailed, and nothing further occurred that week to occasion me alarm. Martha had written to London for the money, and was confident it would arrive in time to enable me to keep the promise I had given.

On the Sunday I attended as usual my class in the village school, and afterwards walked from thence to the church with Mrs. Hurst. As we entered the churchyard, I observed a tall, showily-dressed man, lounging against the porch. As we passed him, he audaciously raised his hat, and as he replaced it on his head, stared impudently in my face.

I had never fully seen the countenance of the man Jasper, but I felt instinctively that he stood before me. He was, as I have said, tall, and, as far as regarded features and complexion, might be denominated handsome; but the expression of his face was of such a repulsive character, that I turned my eyes from his look of bold, impudent recognition, with feelings of terror and shame.

As I entered the church, I was compelled to pass so close to him, that my dress actually brushed against him. To my horror, the wretch seized my hand, and grasped it tightly for an instant in his own.

It was with burning cheeks, and a heart beating with hatred against my persecutor, that I knelt and implored God's blessing on the prayers I was about to offer Him. When I arose and took my seat by the side of my mother, I observed that Mr. Hurst, who had just entered the reading-desk, was looking with evident surprise in the direction of the pew in which we sat. As I arose at the words, "I will arise and go to my father"— words my mother never heard without emotion—I became conscious that the man who had insulted me so grossly as I entered the church was in the seat immediately behind me, and during the time I was standing leant over the back of our pew in such a manner as enabled him to stare impudently in my face. How I longed for the termination of that morning's service, and yet how I dreaded lest I might, in quitting the church, again come in contact with the wretch behind me.

It was our custom to linger in the churchyard till joined by Mr. and Mrs. Hurst, and then walk with them as far as our *route* lay together. On this particular morning, on the plea of not feeling well, I entreated my mother to hasten home at once.

At the gate of the churchyard, through which only one person could pass at a time, stood the object of my fear. This time he did not attempt to touch me, but as I followed my mother through the wicket, he whispered, "You are prettier by daylight than I expected, Nelly."

"Did that bold-looking stranger speak to

you?" asked my mother, looking at my flushed face with surprise.

"He certainly muttered something as I passed, mamma."

"I wonder who he is, Nelly?" was her answer. "I am sure he must be a bad man by the expression of his face. How insolently he behaved in church, leaning forward in such a manner that he might gaze in your face. I hope he is not likely to remain long in the neighbourhood."

Mr. and Mrs. Hurst joined us before we reached the path leading to our home, and my mother, evidently uneasy at the man's insolence to me, immediately inquired if the impertinent stranger was known to them.

"No; I never saw him till to-day," said the Vicar. "Why do you ask?"

My mother replied by mentioning the annoyance he had occasioned us in church, and expressed a hope that he would not remain in the vicinity.

"He certainly has not a very prepossessing countenance, Mrs. Travers, and I should not like any of my female friends to meet him unprotected, for he appears perfectly capable of annoying them, so, Nelly, don't go rambling about by yourself of an evening."

He gave me a quick glance of intelligence as he spoke, and I felt the degrading conviction that he associated my absence from home, a few evenings back, in some manner with this man.

The dreaded, yet anxiously looked-for Wednesday arrived, without my having seen or heard further of my tormentors. Martha had received a cheque for the money, drawn on the bank at W——, and furnished with it I proceeded, at ten o'clock, to the bottom of the garden. My nurse implored me to wait a little later, that she might be able to accompany me; but fearful any delay might induce the woman to fulfil her threat of seeking my mother, I refused her request.

With the cheque tightly grasped in my hand, I hurried to the bottom of the garden. As I approached the spot where I could discern the forms of two persons, I perceived that one of them was on my side of the wall.

It was the man, and with quick steps he advanced to meet me.

"My friend was afraid you would not come, my dear," said he, and that we might have the trouble of going to the house before we had the pleasure of seeing you."

The wretch attempted to take my hand as he spoke, but indignation mastered fear, and I said, "If you do not instantly place yourself on the other side of the wall, I will scream for assistance—I have friends within call."

"Come back, Jasper, and don't be a fool," said the woman, sternly; and with a muttered oath he obeyed her command. "There, now that you have your own way," said she, harshly, "tell me, have you brought the money?"

"Yes, here it is."

"Is it a bank note?" inquired she, as she felt the paper.

"No; it is a cheque on the bank at W——, twelve miles off. It is payable to bearer—you will have no difficulty in getting the money."

They whispered together for a moment, and then the woman said—

"If there *is* any difficulty you will repent it to the last hour of your existence! If not, I have done with you for the present!"

"But I have not!" said the man, and made a movement as if to cross the wall.

Before he could do so, I fled from the spot, and the next instant was in Martha's arms, who had come in search of me.

It was some time after these events before I recovered my usual composure. I seldom went out alone, and never passed the corner where I had met the woman in the lane without a shudder; but when Christmas arrived, and I was still left unmolested, my cheerfulness returned, and I ventured to hope I might never more behold those I feared.

Mr. Lancester and his son were to spend this festival with us. My young brothers, too, were expected home, and my heart was gladdened at the prospect of their arrival. They had passed the summer vacation in travelling with the gentleman under whose care they were placed, and nearly a twelvemonth had passed since we had seen them.

I don't believe any human being could be happier than my sister was at this period. She was now able, with Martha's assistance, to get up and down the stairs; and though still compelled to recline many hours daily on a sofa, she could move, without pain or difficulty, from room to room. Her engagement to Gerald was openly acknowledged, and he prognosticated that by the following summer she would be able to quit home and nurse, and trust herself to a husband's care.

"I don't know, Esther, what we shall do without you," said my mother, when the probability of her leaving us was first spoken of. "I only hope no Gerald will come and take my Nelly from me, though, I suppose, it is what I must expect to happen!"

"Nelly never means to marry; she means to stay always at home with you."

"She must," said Esther, laughing, "if she waits till a Gerald arrives to claim her. I cannot admit there is another to be found."

Gerald had recently resigned his appointment in the army, and immediately after his marriage was to take his bride abroad for some months. On their return, he was to commence practice in London as a consulting surgeon; and my brother Walter, now a fine youth of fifteen, was to become one of his pupils, and reside in his family during the time he was studying the profession his admiration for Gerald had determined him to select. Edmund was yet too young to decide on his future career. They were both high-spirited boys, and their arrival at home diffused happiness throughout the house.

Gerald and his father arrived on Christmas eve; and, as after dinner, with Esther once more amongst us, we drew our chairs to the fire, and the laugh, and the jest, and the affectionate remark went round the circle, it seemed impossible to believe that death, sickness, and misery, had visited us so recently!

The next morning was as bright and sparkling as a Christmas morning should be. All nature appeared rejoicing at the return of that blessed day, on which angels sang of joy in heaven, peace, and goodwill towards men. Summer, in its brightest garb, never decked the earth more beautifully than it was dressed that day. The frost had covered every tree, shrub, and blade of grass in a mantle of glittering silver; while from the tall branches of the large oaks which sheltered the back of the house, and from every projecting ledge, icicles, like precious stones, sparkled in the sun's rays, reflecting every colour of the rainbow. The birds chirrupped merrily as, clustering on the twigs of the tall hollies, they pecked at the brilliant berries which were provided bountifully for their sustenance; and the clear, frosty air brought musically and cheerily to our ears the sound of the church bells.

All was bright and cheering, and the happy voices and ringing laughter of my young brothers seemed as if they were offering a defiance to care and melancholy.

Esther was, that blessed day, for the first time since her accident, to enter God's house to thank him for all His mercies vouchsafed her.

My mother and Martha were to accompany her. Mr. Lancester, Gerald, my brothers, and myself, set off early, in order that we might be ready to assist her from the carriage which had been ordered for her conveyance.

Our walk was a merry one. Walter and Edmund amused themselves in making slides by the wayside, and insisted on teaching me how to glide over them. To my own surprise and satisfaction, I accomplished this feat without a tumble; but when Gerald's foot slipped, and he measured his length on the road, the laughter which followed his downfall—and in which the discomfited knight heartily joined—was loud enough to have issued from the lungs of a boarding school of boys.

I don't think a happier party entered God's house that day, to offer up praises and thanksgivings for the mercies granted them. And as I knelt between my mother and sister—the one almost miraculously restored to health; the other, if not happy, at least free from any present anxiety—I thanked God, from the depths of my heart, that I had been able to keep from them the knowledge of Henry's guilt and his fatal connexion with those who had occasioned such misery to myself—misery for which I was repaid a hundredfold in beholding the tranquillity of my mother and the happiness of Esther and my brothers. What a different C ristmas would it have proved to all, had not Martha afforded me the means of bribing to silence her who had such fearful means of revenge?

I have often wondered at the elasticity with which my spirits rose after any calamity. Who that had seen me that Christmas-day, could have imagined the sorrows through which I had passed in the seventeen years of my life? Still less, that the causes from which they had arisen were yet in existence, and liable at any moment to overwhelm me with fresh trials.

I have often thought how false was the idea intended to be conveyed by the classical fable of the sword suspended over the head of Damocles. Had he worn the crown of

Dionysius a little longer he would have lost his fear of its descent.

One hung over my own head by the slightest thread which could sustain it—the will of a cruel, unscrupulous woman. Yet each day that passed diminished my perception of its presence.

And is it not so with thousands who walk abroad with cheerful looks and erect mien; who rise in the morning with the knowledge that the weapon of destruction, which has so long overshadowed them, may fall and crush them before the night arrives?

Yet such persons "eat, drink, and are merry," and often leave as a legacy to their descendants the sword which has so innocently threatened their own existence. Even as our first father left the most terrible one of all suspended over the head of every human being from the cradle to the grave.

I do not believe it was from any selfish cause that I quickly rallied from the effects of the trials which lately had assailed me. I suppose a naturally vivacious temperament must have done much towards producing such a result, but I think the real cause was my love for my mother and sister. For their sakes, I acted promptly when it was necessary to keep anything from their knowledge which I knew would pain them; and when the pressure was removed from my mind, the necessity of maintaining my usual demeanour, in order that I might not betray my secret, acted beneficially on my spirits, and soon allowed my assumed cheerfulness to become reality.

It is true, for months after I had received that terrible blow I remained nervous and miserable; but the shock I that night sustained, added to the physical injury, had, for the time, completely prostrated my mind; and I did not revive till removed from the place where I lived in constant dread of my brother's return.

The sword was visible to me as long as I remained where I had first beheld it.

It was long since we had passed a Christmas so merrily as the first we spent at Brookfields. Mrs. Hurst had many cheerful gatherings at the Vicarage, and we likewise participated in the gaieties of the neighbourhood. There was a ball at Mrs. Summerdale's, the "county" lady of the vicinity, at which, *chaperoned* by Mrs. Hurst, I was to make my *début* as a grown-up young lady; and in order that I might present a brilliant appearance, Esther's thoughts and Esther's fingers were more occupied in my behalf than Gerald quite approved of.

Too soon those bright days passed away. Walter and Edmund returned to town with Mr. Lancester and Gerald, and the home-life became quiet as before. If Esther's health continued to improve, it was settled she was to become the wife of Gerald in the following August; and although when he left us it was only the middle of February, the thoughts of mother, sister, and nurse were occupied in preparing the *trousseau*, which, said Martha, would require to be very extensive, as, in consequence of Miss Esther's very long illness, she did not possess a single dress beyond the wrappers she still continued to wear. I was, therefore, to proceed to London with Martha, soon after Gerald left us, and purchase some of the materials required for the purpose. I was to be allowed a holiday of a week, which was to be spent at Mr. Lancester's; and my mother and Esther were to pass the period of our absence at the Vicarage. It was, therefore, without anxiety on their account, I quitted home on a bright morning, the latter end of February; and after a drive of five miles to the station with Mr. Hurst, started in the train for London.

CHAPTER XIII.

I HAD no time for reflection of any kind during the time I was with Mr. Lancester. My mornings were passed in the delightful employment of inspecting silks, laces, and muslins; and my evenings in visiting the various places of amusement which my kind friends considered would afford me pleasure. Indeed, I was treated in this respect, both by Gerald and his father, like a spoiled child home for the holidays : their whole occupation appeared to consist in catering for my entertainment. Two days before I was to leave them they engaged a box at one of the theatres, in order that I might view the glories of a wonderful pantomime with which I was certain to be delighted.

Now I would much rather have remained quietly at home on that evening. Unaccustomed to excitement—at least of a pleasurable nature—I felt weary of the incessant whirl in which the last few days had been passed; and then, though I did not like to say so, for fear of mortifying my friends, I really did not like pantomimes.

When at the theatre, however, I tried to laugh as much as was expected at the absurd and noisy scenes which constitute the merit of such entertainments. But I was heartily glad when it was all over, and I found myself slowly following the stream of persons who were, apparently, as eager as myself to quit the scene of their late amusement.

To reach the entrance of the theatre, we had to pass down a narrow passage, divided only by a low partition from that which led from the pit. In the middle of that we were detained a short time, while some of the crowd in front passed through the doors.

While waiting to advance, Gerald whispered to me—

" Nelly, do you know that man who is

staring at you so intently from the other side?"

I turned my head quickly, and saw a man rudely and hastily pushing his way through the crowd which surrounded him.

"It can be no one I am acquainted with," said I, "for I do not know a single person in London but yourselves."

"Then you have made a conquest, Nelly —though, I fear, not a very reputable one— for his look was certainly expressive of admiration. He was a good-looking fellow, too, in an impudent, vulgar style of good looks."

Gerald's words filled my mind with a vague kind of dread. Was it possible that the man he had observed could be the one I had such reason to dread; and if so, would he dare molest me while under the protection of Mr. Lancester?

Martha, however, laughed at my apprehensions when I confided them to her, and said I must not be surprised at people's staring at me in such public places; and, ashamed to lay so much stress on the gaze of a passing stranger, I dismissed it from my mind, and the next morning, if I thought of it at all, it was only to laugh at my folly.

The last day I was to spend in town was devoted to the business which brought me there. I had despatched patterns of various articles for my sister's selection, and had now to give my final directions respecting them. Mr. Lancester had engaged a carriage for my use during the time I was his guest, and it was quite dark when I entered it for the last time at the door of a shop in Bond Street, where my last purchases were made.

When I met Mr. Lancester and Gerald at dinner, they both congratulated me on my looks, and the latter declared that spending money was evidently the most delightful of all occupations to a young lady.

"And I should think," answered I, "that earning it must be the most delightful of employments to a man, for I have observed that an idle one is the most wretched of mortals."

"Very true, Nelly. We do feel pleasure in working hard, that those we love may have the enjoyment of spending easily, but then we expect something in return beyond that of seeing them arrayed in purple and fine linen. I shall insist, as soon as my marital authority commences, on Esther's learning by heart the speech of Katherine to her sister and Hortensio's widow. It is the best manual of a wife's duties that ever was written."

"Certainly," said I, "it will be very comical to see Esther turned into a bootjack for your benefit. I am afraid you will not find her quite so submissive as you imagine."

Just as I was about to leave the dining-room, a servant informed me that a young person from Messrs. A——'s, in Bond Street, was waiting to see me. Supposing it was some one called for further directions respecting a dress I had ordered, I desired her to be shown into the breakfast-room, where I went to meet her.

The tables, the chairs, the sofa, and every available place where parcels could be deposited, were occupied with my numerous purchases, and, as I entered, I perceived that one of them—the largest—which contained silks for dresses, was unfastened, and its contents were being inspected by the young woman waiting to see me. She turned her head at my approach, and, to my dismay, I found myself once more face to face with the woman Rachel.

"You do not appear pleased to see me, Miss Nelly," said she, in a jeering tone, as pale as death I recoiled from her touch. "Did you suppose I should not pay my respects to you when I discovered you were in London. Jasper happened luckily to see you last night at the theatre, but could not manage to trace you home. I knew, however, that Regent Street and its neighbourhood were the decoys for rustics like you, and you have been tracked to-day from shop to shop, though it was only at the last one I succeeded in learning your address; and I immediately posted off to assure you of my joy at so unexpectedly meeting you."

During the time she was speaking, I was bracing myself to hear with calmness the purport of her visit. That she was come for the purpose of annoying me I felt certain; nor did she leave me long in ignorance of her motive for seeking me.

In answer to my question of why she had done so, she replied by asking me, in a tone of mock politeness, to take a chair, at the same time seating herself on the sofa. As I remained standing, she continued, "Oh! as you please; we will then come to business at once. I unfortunately require fifty pounds immediately, and naturally look to the sister of Henry Travers to furnish me with it."

The woman's cool impudence roused my anger, and for the time caused me to forget the fatal power she possessed over me. I replied, indignantly, "I have not fifty pounds, and if I had, I would not allow you to frighten me out of one shilling of it."

The look of almost good-humoured audacity her face had hitherto worn, suddenly gave place to the expression of terrible ferocity I had seen it wear before. Rising from the sofa on which she had been indolently lolling, she approached me, and in a low, passionate voice, said,

"If you dare speak to me again like that,

I will compel you to entreat my pardon on your knees, you wretched little worm! Do you think you can defy me? Not got money indeed! I should think you must have plenty to be able to buy such things as these." And she pointed to the contents of the parcel she had unfastened. "But if you really have spent all your money, I will give you five minutes to consider how you can procure it. Only make up your mind that it *must* be found, and you will find the task easy I have no doubt."

My temporary courage had quite vanished by this time, and I felt almost grateful for the short respite afforded me to collect my thoughts. I rapidly came to the conclusion that I must adopt one of two courses—either defy my enemy, and call Mr. Lancester to my assistance, or again endeavour to bribe her to silence. But how was I to do so? And even if I could, what security had I that I should not again and again be called on to satisfy the rapacity of these harpies?

While I remained still hesitating how I ought to act, a hand was laid on my shoulder, and, looking up, I saw the bright eyes of the woman fixed on my face.

"Well, have you decided?—the five minutes are gone."

"You will obtain no more money from me!" said I, firmly. "I have resolved to tell my friends of your persecutions, and of the mode by which you extorted it from me before. Do and say what you will, I am determined to free myself from your importunities for the future!"

I half expected she would have offered me violence when I thus defied her; but, to my astonishment, she dropped me a low curtsey, and thanked me for my kind intentions towards her—adding, with an insolent smile, "I see I did wrong not to bring Jasper with me. You would not prove so obstinate if he was here!"

The very sound of that man's name caused my heart to beat with increased violence; but determined she should not see my alarm, I walked towards the bell for the purpose of summoning assistance.

She saw my intention, and placed herself in my path.

"It does not matter," said I, in answer to her look of intimidation, "I have only to raise my voice, and my friends will hasten to me."

She stood for a few moments irresolute, and then said—

"Well, for this once you have the advantage. Plume yourself on it as much as you please, it will not be long your's!"

She then opened the door, and as she was about to quit the room, Gerald, who was on the point of entering, stood aside for her to pass; and then looking at me, and observing my pale face, he exclaimed—

"Why, Nelly, your long conversation with that dressmaker has fatigued you more than all your day's work! I have come to tell you we are waiting for you to pour out the coffee."

As soon as I could make my escape, I imparted to Martha all I had gone through since I had seen her just previous to the dinner, and asked her opinion as to the prudence of at once informing Mr. Lancester of what had occurred; for now that I had thrown down the gauntlet, I did not doubt I should be soon again assailed.

She hesitated before she answered me, and then acknowledged that, frightful as was my liability to be harassed by these people, and hopeless as it appeared to satisfy their demands, she dreaded the effects of an open rupture with them, and reminded me of what I had selfishly overlooked, that Esther's marriage would most probably never take place if she was acquainted with her brother's guilt. She would refuse to bring disgrace into the home of an honourable man.

I knew that Martha was right; that my sister would be firm in her refusal of Gerald, if she knew of the power these vile wretches boasted over their wretched victim.

What should we do? We asked each other this question repeatedly. At last the coward's refuge—delay—was resolved on. We might hear no more of Rachel and her confederate. Alarmed at my threat of informing my friends of their persecutions, and well knowing Henry was beyond their reach, they might not molest me again.

And with this faint hope for the future, I determined to keep secret all that related to the past.

It was always a relief to me in any emergency when I had decided on a course of action. And now that I had done so in this instance, I was able to assist Martha in packing our various purchases ready for departure early the following morning. We were in the breakfast-room, occupied in this manner, when a letter was given me, with the intimation that the person who delivered it would call in half-an-hour for an answer.

At the first glance of the paper within the envelope, I uttered an exclamation of surprise and horror.

In my hand was the evidence that Rachel had not spoken falsely in declaring the fearful power she held over me.

The letter was in the well-known writing of my brother! Of that brother whom I imagined separated thousands of miles from his evil companions, endeavouring to gain an honourable competence, and striving to blot out the remembrance of his former errors by his present exemplary conduct!

I could scarcely credit the evidence of my eyesight—but, alas! there was no room for doubt.

"Nelly, I conjure you by all you hold dear in this world or sacred in the next, to give Rachel the money she desires! I have been in England for some time, bankrupt of all that my mother had bestowed. To Rachel it is owing I am not now in a felon's prison; but I shall be delivered up to the punishment I merit, should you provoke her by resistance to her demands! Once more, Nelly, save me for our mother's sake!"

This letter was not signed, but I knew it was written by him who, from my earliest recollection, had been the cause of shame and misery in my home!

Hesitation was now at an end. I must buy the silence of Henry's associates, and endeavour, if possible, to rescue him from their toils. I had still part of the money my mother had given me for the purchase of

Esther's wedding clothes, but not sufficient to satisfy the demand of the woman.

Alas! ought that wedding ever to take place? Ought I not to let Esther free from his engagement the man who was about to give her an honourable name, and who would do so in ignorance that at any moment it might be assailed with disgrace?

Have any of those who may peruse these pages ever known the dull, tranquil feeling which succeeds a period of uncertainty? When the hope deferred has become the hope annihilated; while the mind, stunned by the shock, is incapable of realizing the consequences which must result from its extinction. If they have not, let them pray God to spare them its knowledge.

Such a state was mine after I read that letter. All feeling was crushed within my heart: hope and fear were alike dead. The sword had fallen, but it had struck me with the blunted edge; and had numbed, instead of lacerating me.

It was fortunate, for the preservation of my reason, that Jasper Coxe was the person who, within an hour, was ushered into the room "as the person who had come for an answer to the letter." The sight of this detested man roused me from the lethargy which was stealing over my faculties.

He waited a short time after his entrance before he spoke, as if expecting Martha would leave the room; but when he perceived I intended her to remain, he said, carelessly—

"Just as you please! If you don't mind people's knowing of Harry's misfortune, I am sure I don't! I am come upon business to-night, and have no time for love-making!"

"How dare you speak to Miss Ellen like that?" said Martha, confronting him, with flashing eyes, and hand uplifted as if to strike him.

"Hold your tongue, old woman!" answered he, with perfect good humour. "Do you suppose it is the first time this pretty rosebud has heard me talk of love to her? We have had delightful moonlight meetings that I'll be bound she never told you about!" And the man winked impudently at me as he uttered the words. "But, as I said, to-night I come on business. Have you got the cash ready for Rachel, or will you take a pleasant walk to-morrow and visit your brother in her Majesty's commodious mansion called Newgate? It will hurt our feelings to put an old friend in such quarters, but it is purely a commercial transaction—an affair of pounds, shillings, and pence, my little Nelly! So make your choice—only be quick about it!"

I did not betray the slightest emotion, either of fear or anger. I did not wince under the insults the man poured on my head, but, with a calm voice, answered—

"Tell me first when and where I can see my brother."

"If he wants to see you, I suppose he'll look you up himself. You won't find him out through me. If you want to send him an extra fifty, I'll take charge of it for him, and see he gets it safe!"

I emptied the contents of my purse on the table. There was thirty-six pounds remaining of the hundred my mother had given me for my purchases, some of which I was not to pay for till they were sent to Brookfields.

The man took it up, counted it, and then said, "This won't do—I must have twenty-four more!"

"Why, you only demand fifty," said Martha; "it is only fourteen pounds short of that sum."

"Quite correct, ma'am—you ought to have been brought up an accountant! But I charge ten pounds for my trouble in coming here to-night. Indeed, twenty is the proper fee; but I have thrown off ten for the pleasure of seeing my charming Nelly!"

Faint and sick with despair, I looked helplessly to Martha for aid; nor did I seek it in vain.

"You shall have that sum," said she, "in a week from this time, if you will wait till then."

He hesitated a short time, and then said, "Ah! my good nature will be the ruin of me some day! But if you promise to let me have the money in a week, I will bear the brunt of Rachel's temper for going back without it. But where am I to come for it—here?"

"No; we return to Brookfields to-morrow."

"Then I will indulge myself with a mouthful of country air, and a meeting at the old time and place with my charming Nelly, who little knows all I endure on her account, from the jealousy of Rachel. Won't you shake hands before we part? Oh! very well; perhaps you won't be quite so shy this night week."

And with an insolent nod, he followed Martha from the room.

I was hardly conscious of all the insults I had received from him; my thoughts were filled with the dreadful intelligence of which he had been the bearer.

Henry in England! In the power of those who boasted of their ability to deliver him up to a shameful punishment, and who only deferred carrying their threats into execution as long as I could furnish them with the money they extorted from my fears.

One thought—one burning wish above all others—haunted me. Could I but discover their victim, and rescue him from their power?

Wild thoughts, vain wishes! I could do nothing but return to my mother, and as long as possible spare her the agony I was experiencing myself.

The following morning I left Streatham. Gerald accompanied me to the station; but he was too much occupied in instructing me with innumerable messages to Esther—his thoughts too much filled with his own happy future—to see more than symptoms of fatigue in my dull, heavy eyes and abstracted manner.

There were several persons in the carriage in which he had placed me, so that I was unable to converse with Martha; but when seated in the one which was to convey me from the station, she entreated me to try and hide from my mother the wretchedness I felt.

"If you could only have a good cry, dear," said this true friend, "you would feel better."

But I knew she was wrong. If once I allowed my feelings to overpower me, I should not be able to restrain them more. So with the same calm, dull look I met my mother and sister, as they waited in the porch of the door to welcome me.

My heart ached as I looked at Esther's face, radiant with love, and joy, and hope, as she stood that afternoon with the sun shining on her beautiful golden hair and her eyes sparkling with animation. She knew the cargo of loving words with which I was freighted, and that more than would be committed to my memory would be in the letter of which I was sure to be the bearer. How soon might tears of bitter anguish stain those cheeks which now blushed with innocent delight as she received the words of affection I delivered to her from her betrothed?

After tea, all the packages were brought in and opened by Martha; and when everything had been admired and approved, my mother said, "How much have you brought back in your purse, Nelly?"

It was very strange, but till this question was asked, I had not remembered that I must give an account of my stewardship; and I turned sick at the sudden thought that I had no means of accounting for such a large portion of the sum entrusted to me.

I turned a scared look on Martha, who promptly came to my aid.

"We have all the bills up-stairs, ma'am, but Miss Nelly is too tired to go over them to-night; but when you see them, I don't fear you will think we have been extravagant."

"I think my Nelly has managed every thing admirably, with the exception of returning with such a pale face. I shall scold Gerald for not taking better care of you. Go to bed, dear, and look more like yourself to-morrow."

I was very thankful to find myself alone. Now for the first time, during the last four-and-twenty hours, I was able to reflect. One thought was predominant above all others—above even my fears for my mother—my apprehensions for Henry. It was the conviction that Esther's marriage would not take place. But what mattered that? She would die of shame and grief when acquainted with all that must soon be revealed.

"Oh, my sister!" cried I, in the anguish of my heart, "my dear, dear sister, would that the sacrifice of my life could assure the happiness of your's!"

With the first glimpse of day, I left my room, and wandered from the garden into the road which led towards the Vicarage. I had no motive for so doing, no knowledge even of the way I strayed; but the cool morning air blowing in my face assuaged the burning pain in my head; and I went on and on till I came to the turning where I had first met the terrible Rachel. I passed it, for the first time since I had done so, without fear. I had now nothing to dread, should soon have nothing to conceal. I must account to my mother for the missing money, and how could I do so but by a relation of the truth?

Absorbed in my painful reflections, I reached the Vicarage; and still, with the same purposeless steps, opened the gate, and walked to the house. Early as it was, Mr. Hurst was writing in his study, the windows of which looked out on the lawn. He saw me as I passed, and directly was by my side.

"Good God! Nelly," he exclaimed, "what is wrong with you? Your mother—Esther! speak, are they ill?"

I tried to answer him; but, as usual with me, violent emotion deprived me for the time of the power of articulating a word. I felt as if the earth was reeling to and fro— I tried to clutch at Mr. Hurst to support me —and was conscious of nothing more till I found myself in his mother's sitting-room, extended on the sofa, and Mr. Neave, the surgeon of the village, standing by me.

"She is better now," were the first words I heard. "You must keep her very quiet for some hours. I will call on Mrs. Travers as I return, and tell her she will pass the morning with you. I will be careful not to alarm her on Miss Ellen's account."

For more than two hours I remained almost without the power of thought; but as the stupor which succeeded the sudden faintness which had seized me, passed away, the tears flowed through my closed lids, and betrayed to my watchful friend that something more than accidental indisposition had occasioned my present state.

"Tell me, my dear girl," said she, tenderly, "what it is which has caused this affliction. Confide it to one who loves you, and whose counsels may assist to alleviate it."

My long suppressed tears now burst forth without control, and I sobbed with hysterical violence in the arms of my terrified friend.

"I will tell you all," said I, when able to speak coherently; "I can no longer bear the weight of my secret wretchedness, and you will direct me how best to impart it to my mother and Esther."

I told her all the particulars of the dreadful night when my mother's house was robbed; of my interview with the woman in the lane; and all I had since endured from her persecution; and then took from my bosom the dreadful letter I had received the night before I quitted London. The awful uncertainty respecting the crimes of which they accused Henry was not the least part of my misery.

What could he have done, which enabled these miscreants to exert such authority over him?

Mrs. Hurst was dreadfully shocked at the story I related, and was as unable as myself to decide on the proper course to adopt.

"Let me tell my husband, Nelly, he is wiser than either of us, and will know how to act for the best. He shall come to you, and together we will decide what course should be taken. It is certain you must no longer submit to the threats and extortions of these people. Better at once to brave the worst, than to live in constant fear of it. I will go and send Philip to you directly."

I was too ill to resist her wishes, even had I felt inclined. Worn out by want of rest, and exhausted by violent emotion, I fell into a heavy slumber which must have been of some duration.

When I awaked, Mr. Hurst was sitting by the sofa.

"Jane is gone to your mother's, Nelly," said he, "and deputed me to watch you during her absence. She has told me something, my child, of this affair. You must tell me yourself all that appertains to it, and do not doubt but we will contrive to baffle the schemes of these abandoned wretches, and deliver your brother from their power."

When I had related my sad story, he blamed me gently for not having at once called on him for assistance.

"But this terrible letter! Is it not possible it may be a forgery? The people from whom you received it are, no doubt, well acquainted with your brother's writing. May they not have imitated it for the purpose of frightening you, and thus the more easily induce you to comply with their demands?"

A gleam of hope seemed, for the moment, to illumine my heart, as I listened to this suggestion. I took the letter from his hand, and eagerly scanned the formation of every letter. Alas! there was no ground for disbelief. Henry's writing was very peculiar: owing to the fracture of his right thumb, when a child, he was unable to hold the pen in the usual manner, although he could use it with great rapidity.

This gave a marked singularity to his writing, which it would have been very difficult to have imitated.

I returned the paper to Mr. Hurst with a heavy sigh, and an assurance that it was indeed written by my brother.

I spent the morning with the elder Mrs. Hurst, who was taken into our confidence, and it was by her advice that we finally resolved to act.

"You may be quite sure, my dear, that if your brother is residing with those wicked persons, and has committed any crime of which they are cognisant, that they are implicated in it, and are in as much dread of detection as he is.

"Go with this child, Philip, to the place where she has promised to meet them with the money. Tell them not one farthing shall they receive till they reveal the place of this unhappy young man's concealment; and if they refuse, or attempt to alarm you by threats of the vengeance they can take on their victim, declare your determination to have them apprehended for extorting money from Nelly by false representations. Rely on it, they will be alarmed at the very idea of being given into custody on such a charge, and will give you the information you demand rather than run the risk of being examined before a magistrate. When you have thus discovered the wretched boy's hiding-place, it will be time to determine how you must act towards his guilty confederates."

"My dear mother," said Mr. Hurst, "I am almost ready to exclaim with Shylock, 'a Daniel come to judgment!' We will follow your advice to the letter, and I feel convinced that good must result from doing so. And now, Nelly, my child, cheer up; by God's help, we shall release your brother from the clutches of these harpies, and then their power of tormenting you must cease. Meet your mother and Esther with a smiling face, for they must remain in ignorance of all the trouble which you, for their sakes, have so bravely borne!"

"But, Mr. Hurst," asked I, "what am I

to do about the money? Martha will not get it for a week, and my mother will be surprised if I do not furnish an account of it."

"Be easy on that point, Nelly. You shall take home with you to-night what you require for the purpose, only keep from her knowledge that which has occurred, and all will yet be well."

I passed the remainder of that day in almost happy tranquillity. The more I reflected on the counsel of Mrs. Hurst, the more I was convinced of the justice of her surmises respecting the fears Rachel and the man Jasper would feel at the prospect of being taken before a magistrate.

Martha took as hopeful a view as myself of the benefit which must attend the interference of Mr. Hurst. And that night I forgot, for several hours, in refreshing sleep, the events which for two nights and days had overwhelmed me with anxiety.

CHAPTER XIV.

Very fortunately, during the six days I had to pass before the evening of the one on which that dreaded meeting was to take place, my mother and sister were too much occupied in cutting out and arranging work to observe that I was more silent than usual; but if I did not talk, I worked incessantly, in the hope that constant employment would assist in banishing reflection.

Esther was to be no exception to the generality of brides. She was to be furnished with a wardrobe sufficiently ample to supply her wants for years to come; and I was very thankful that the preparations for her wedding were likely to occupy my mother's thoughts for some time, and thus prevent them from dwelling on the long silence of my brother Henry.

I passed the day on which I was to purchase the silence of his vile associate at the Vicarage, and shortly before the appointed time walked with Mr. Hurst to the spot where I had formerly met him. We reached it just as the clock was striking the hour. Minute after minute passed away, yet no sound of footsteps met our ears, no figure started up through the gloom, to claim the fulfilment of the promise I had made that night week.

With slow and noiseless steps we paced up and down the path from which we could look into the orchard, scarcely venturing to speak lest we should lose the first intimation of the approach of him I at once longed, yet dreaded to behold.

The night was bitterly cold, but so still, that the faintest sound was distinctly audible; I could even hear the beating of my own heart as I stood gazing into the darkness, expecting each moment to behold the form and hear the mocking tones of that detested man.

My mind was so wholly absorbed with the hopes and fears regarding the result of this interview, that I was unconscious of the lapse of time, till Mr. Hurst roused me by saying, "Nelly, you must now go in; the chimes have gone the half hour, and we will wait no longer."

"I cannot go—indeed I cannot go yet!" I replied. "He will come, and not finding me here, will do as the woman threatened, and force himself into my mother's presence."

"I will not allow you to remain longer, Nelly. I do not believe you have any further ground for apprehension. My first surmise respecting the letter was correct. It is a vile forgery, concocted for the purpose of extorting money from your fears. They will not venture to molest you more, now that they are aware you have acquainted your friends with the whole story—and they have discovered that fact from tracking us here to-night. I only wish," added he, raising his voice, "that this man had been impudent enough to have met us, and, as I have no doubt he is lurking somewhere here, I shall look narrowly as I return through the lanes, and endeavour to discover his hiding-place."

I entered the house with my mind lightened of its heavy load. I suffered myself to believe Mr. Hurst was right, that the letter was never written by Henry, and that having watched us from the Vicarage, they were aware their power over my fears was at an end.

This hope became certainty as weeks passed, and I heard no further tidings from the woman or my brother. My health and spirits revived as the time went on, and once more I dared look to the future without dread. Spring came and went, and summer had advanced nearly to the end of July, and still nothing more was heard by me of Henry.

Esther had continued to gain strength, and Gerald triumphantly declared she wanted nothing but one winter in Italy to be as well as before her accident, and boasted that when he brought her home in the following May, Martha would not know her nursling.

My sister had insisted on telling Gerald all the particulars of Henry's misconduct as far as they were known to herself.

"It is very painful," said she, when she informed me of her intentions—"it is very painful to have such things to disclose of my brother, but it would be both weak and wicked to become the wife of an honourable man, and leave him in ignorance of that which might cause him afterwards to reproach me with duplicity, and to regret he had bestowed his name on a woman nearly allied to one whose conduct, if known, would reflect disgrace on all connected with him. I may feel humiliated by disclosing a brother's errors, but my husband shall never have reason to accuse me of deceiving him."

Ah! thought I, there is little danger to be apprehended, that anything you can impart to Gerald will cause him to love you one iota the less, or even to refuse Henry's hand as a brother, if he were here to offer it; but if he knew all that I could tell him—that he had committed crimes which rendered him amenable to the laws of his country—that he had been the friend and associate of midnight robbers and assassins—would his love be strong enough to brave the obloquy of such a connexion?

The wedding was to take place in the first week in August. A fortnight before the time, Walter and Edmund arrived at home. Walter was to appear at the ceremony in the dignified character of father, and give the bride away. Edmund was equally proud at being selected to officiate as best man to the bridegroom, while Maude Headley—a niece of Mr. Lancester's—and myself were to be the bridesmaids.

In the midst of all the bustle attending the preparations for this, the first festival I ever remembered in our family, I hoped my mother would be too much, and happily occupied, to think with anxiety of Henry; but I was deceived. When Walter allowed his boyish exultation to appear at being appointed to such an office at his sister's wedding, she said, sadly,

"I wonder he does not feel that his having to act as his brother's proxy ought to be a subject of regret. My poor Henry! no one but his mother remembers that he is an exile striving—perhaps in the midst from his home, of dangers—to blot out the remembrance of his youthful errors."

I do not think ever daughter loved her mother more devotedly than I did mine, yet when she used to accuse me indirectly with unkindness to him whose crimes I had at such fearful suffering to myself kept from her knowledge, and whom, unworthy as he was, I felt was dearer to her than myself, I could not sometimes refrain from thinking her unkind and inconsiderate; and, without reflecting she was ignorant of the reasons I had to dread his return, I more than once answered her words of regret at his absence with some careless remark, expressive of my own conviction that it was better he should be away.

As the day drew nearer and nearer which was to take my dear sister from us, I became nervously uneasy lest some obstacle should arise which might turn the house of joy into the house of mourning. Each arrival of the post was dreaded, for fear it should bring tidings which might hinder the marriage from taking place. Let me, I thought, but be assured of Esther's happiness, and I will never indulge in anticipations of evil again. Oh! that the day were past, and my heart at peace on her account!

It came, and brought no shadow to darken its brightness; all was as unclouded as the brilliant sunshine which poured through the eastern window of the old church, and cast a radiance on the group which clustered round the altar.

Never did bride look more lovely than my sweet sister, never did woman pledge a purer or more loving heart in that holy temple to the man who vowed to love and cherish her for ever.

There was no parade in our quiet home that day. It was not a gay wedding, but it was a tolerably cheerful one. Mr. and Mrs. Hurst returned with us after the ceremony, not to partake of an elaborate breakfast, and listen to unmeaning speeches, but to bid farewell to Gerald and his bride. My mother struggled bravely to hide her sorrow at parting from her best loved daughter, and I tried hard to forget I had for ever lost the friend and companion of my whole life — that Gerald's wife could never be to me the sister Esther of my youth.

Gerald allowed but short time for leave-taking. I felt that affection for us all induced him to hurry his wife away—that the longer the parting was protracted, the more painful it would prove—but when I could no longer discern the carriage which conveyed her from me, I threw my arms round my mother's neck, and wept unchecked on her bosom.

When calm enough to observe it, I was shocked at seeing how very wretched she herself looked. "It is nothing, Nelly," she answered, to my inquiries: "but a mother cannot part from her children without great sorrow."

"I will never leave you, mamma!" cried I; "but, oh! if you could but love me as you do Esther and Henry!"

She looked both pained and surprised at my vehemence. "Why should you doubt my affection for you, Nelly? It is true that your brother and sister have engrossed more of my thoughts than yourself, but have they not stood in greater need of my care? Remember, it is not very long ago since you were the chief cause of my anxiety, and even Esther was neglected for your sake. Think, my child, of the last words addressed to you by your father—I remember them well—he predicted that your eagerness to receive what you considered proofs of affection, would eventually occasion you unhappiness. But now go to our guests; we must not suffer them to think they are uncared or unwished for. I will join you soon, and Esther's wedding-day shall not be rendered gloomy by recollections of the past."

It was utterly impossible that any one could be otherwise than cheerful with such companions as Mr. Lancester, Maude Headley, and my young brothers. They laughed so heartily at my dismal face when I entered the room where they were assembled, that I soon felt ashamed of my selfish regrets, and when my mother joined us at dinner, she appeared surprised to find me the gayest of that merry party. Mr. Lancester and my brothers were to leave us the next morning. My mother had consented that her sons should pass the next twelvemonths in Hanover, and our good friend was to leave England with them in a few days, and see them safely consigned to the care of the gentleman under whose charge they were to remain.

When we were separating for the night, Mr. Lancester asked me to be down early the following morning, as he had something particular to say to me before he left; adding, as he saw my look of alarm at his words—

"Don't look so terrified, Nelly; it is nothing very formidable, though a matter of some consequence to your mother. But you need not let your imagination conjure up anything evil enough to occasion you to sleep less soundly than usual."

I could not avoid feeling that whatever might be the purport of that communication, it was something which would be productive of vexation, or why was it to be kept secret from my mother. Eager to know in what shape evil was now to come, I was in the garden, the following morning, two hours before the breakfast-hour, and waited impatiently for half that time the appearance of my friend.

He did not keep me long in ignorance of the subject he had to discuss.

"I am going, Nelly, to speak to you relative to your mother's affairs. You know the extent of her income, but perhaps you are not aware that the capital from which it was derived has been greatly diminished recently. You, no doubt, remember when the first inroad was made on it; and although it was only for such a small sum as three hundred pounds, it was a great misfortune; for it showed with what facility money could be obtained by your mother, when she required more than her regular income sufficed. Since you have been at Brookfields, your expenses have been much greater than they should in prudence have been.

"Do not interrupt me, Nelly. I know

you have not spent too profusely here. But recollect that heavy expenses are going on at Streatham; that they have, during the last year, increased considerably for Walter and Edmund; and that a large—a very large sum—was appropriated to Henry when he quitted England.

"Your mother has also—contrary to my earnest wishes—spent more than was either necessary or prudent on Esther. Your illness last year was a most unfortunate event, for it compelled her to take the management of her affairs in her own hands; and without the least idea of acting imprudently, she has managed to involve them to a considerable extent. At this time you ought not to allow the whole of your expenditure to exceed five hundred a year; and fully half that sum will be required for some time to come by your brothers, if they are to complete their education, as it is proposed, in Germany."

I was perfectly astonished at this revelation. I knew that my mother had obtained some money recently, independent of her regular resources; but certainly a thousand pounds would cover all that I knew of, including the three hundred advanced through Mr. Bingley. And though I had never heard how much she bestowed on Henry when he left for Canada, I could not believe it could be anything like the amount which Mr. Lancester had told me was withdrawn from the funds.

"What sum did my mother advance Henry?" inquired I.

"Two thousand pounds!"

"Then, Mr. Lancester, you must be mistaken in the amount you say has been spent. I am sure we have not expended more than a thousand pounds in addition to the eight hundred of our income."

"I know that, Nelly; but, unfortunately, when your mother was in London, she went with your brother to some stockbroker, to sell out the sum he required; and was persuaded it would be greatly to her advantage to entrust a few thousands to him, in order, as he expressed it, that by a few lucky turns of the market she might be enabled to replace the sum she had just withdrawn from the funds. I knew nothing of this transaction till a few days ago, when I heard this man had failed for an immense sum, and that your mother's name figured amongst his creditors. When I called at your house at Streatham the day before I left London, Susan gave me an official looking letter to bring down which I instantly recognised as a communication from the assignees of the bankrupt; but I resolved not to sadden our children's wedding by being the bearer of bad tidings.

"Now that you know all this, Nelly, you will see the necessity of retrenchment. You cannot continue to maintain two establishments. If you do not intend to return to the house at Streatham, persuade your mother to find a tenant for it; and that will at once remove all your difficulties. If she consents to do so, I will arrange that she shall have no trouble respecting it.

"And now clear your brow, and let us go in to breakfast. Don't send Walter and Edmund away melancholy. They are both fine fellows, and years should pass over their heads before they know the meaning of the word 'care!'"

I thought, as I looked at their happy faces when I entered the room, where they were seated at breakfast, that there was little fear of their noticing the expression of anxiety on my own. But I wronged their kind hearts by such a supposition. They did observe my depression, although they attributed it to their own departure and my separation from my sister.

"Dear Nell," said Walter, as he passed his arm round my waist, "I am grieved to see you look so sad. You will indeed miss Esther greatly; but cheer up, twelve months will soon pass away and then we shall be home. Edmund and I will write you long long letters about all we see and do. Besides," he added, in a whisper, casting a schoolboy's shy glance of admiration at Maude, "you will have Miss Headley with you for some weeks, and she is so lively and good-tempered, that you will soon recover your spirits."

"Now then, sir!" cried Edmund, at this moment, who had been impatiently watching Mr. Lancester eating his breakfast. "Here's your hat and stick. We shall be too late for the train. The fly has been waiting this half hour. Come along, Walter, we must say good-bye once more to mamma!"

There was a rushing up stairs, which I knew would unsettle my mother's nerves for the day; a few rather boisterous kisses on my own cheek from the boys; an affectionate farewell from Mr. Lancester, and I was left with no one but my mother to love and care for, during twelve long months!

CHAPTER XV.

I HAVE made hitherto but slight mention of Maude Headley, and yet she is to play a prominent part in the after portion of my life.

She was the daughter of Mr. Lancester's only sister, and, at the time she arrived at Brookfields, was between seventeen and eighteen years of age. She would not have been considered pretty at first sight; at least, I did not think her so, as she stood by the side of Esther. She was very short and slight, with a clear, brown complexion; to which exercise, or any pleasurable excitement, brought almost too vivid a colour.

When her face was in repose, I have heard persons remark that her mouth, which was very wide, quite spoiled her appearance; but the teeth were so white and beautifully formed, as fully to compensate for this defect, when talking in the animated and joyous manner which was natural to her, "and when," said Walter, "her dark eyes sparkled and flashed as brilliantly as diamonds in the sunshine."

She has never known a care or sorrow, thought I, as I looked in her bright face and listened to her happy laugh. She can never be more than a fine weather friend. It would be vain to look for help or sympathy from her, in times of affliction or anxiety. I misjudged my new friend as I had done others. The sun gladdens us by its warmth, though its brightness dazzles our eyesight.

Maude's nature was sunny, but I soon discovered it could be clouded when the hearts of those she loved were bowed down by calamity.

Her father had been dead more than two years, but her mother continued to reside in the secluded village of which, for a great number of years, he had been the pastor. Since her widowhood, Mr. Lancester had been urgent in wishing her to leave Baymouth, and reside with him at Streatham; but hitherto she had resisted all his entreaties to do so, although it would have brought her near her only son, who resided in chambers in the Temple.

"Mamma will never leave Baymouth," said Maude one day, when speaking to me concerning her home-life, "and though I do sometimes grumble and say it is dull, yet I love the dear old place too well to wish to exchange it for such a make-believe sort of country existence as Streatham affords. I have heard the sea roar in winter and murmur in summer, ever since I was born, and do not think I could live happily away from its neighbourhood. I have read a great deal of the love of the Swiss for their mountain homes, but I think it can hardly surpass that which those born and nurtured on the coast feel at the sound and sight of the sea. You must go back with me, Nelly, and see how different you will feel as you inhale the pure, bracing air; it will bring fresh life into your frame, fresh hope and joy into your heart."

"Oh!" answered I, ungraciously, for I was rather annoyed at her contemptuous mention of Streatham. "I have seen the sea often enough. I used to go to Brighton every year before Esther was ill, and I did not care much about it."

"Brighton!" answered Maude. "Oh! if you have no remembrances of the sea but those connected with Brighton, I am not surprised at your apathy respecting it. If anything could destroy the poetry of the ocean, it would be the great staring houses and the crowds of people who flock to that place, not to gaze at the sea, but each other. No; I don't care for it myself with the accompaniments of brass bands and gaslights. To love the sea you must behold it as poets have loved to depict it. Could Crabbe have written his glorious lines if he had never beheld it but from the 'King's Road'? Listen! and then remember this is the sea I will show you, and which will dash almost against the wall of the room in which you will sleep :

> 'Various and vast, sublime in all its forms,
> When lull'd by zephyrs and when rous'd by storms.
> Its colours changing, when from clouds and sun,
> Shades after shades upon the surface run.
> Embrown'd and horrid now; and now serene,
> In limpid blue and evanescent green.'"

"Well," said I, when Maude had finished her recitation, "I suppose the colour of the sea is not altered at Brighton because there are plenty of persons to view it. It must be just the same there as at Baymouth."

"No doubt, Nelly; and a storm is a storm whether beheld by the glare of gaslights or by the fitful glimpses of the moon, and yet you look on it with very different feelings. But I will quote my favourite poet again, and then judge for yourself ' of the sublime and beautiful ' :

> ' From parted clouds, the moon her radiance throws
> On the wild waves, and all the danger shows,
> But shows them beaming in her shining vest,
> Terrific splendour, gloom in glory 'drest.
> This for a moment, and then clouds again
> Hide every beam, and fear and darkness reign.

*   *   *   *

But hear we not those sounds? Do lights appear?
I see them not ; the storm alone I hear ;
And as the sailors homeward take their way ;
Men must endure—let us submit and pray.'"

"You are right, Maude," said I, when she had finished speaking, "the sea in all its sublimity is unknown to me. How strange I should never have read a line of the poet who points with such marvellous power its terrific beauty."

"Not at all strange, Nelly—few young ladies do read him; but my father prized him, after Shakespeare and Milton, above all other poets. He was one of our household gods; loved and admired the more, because we were daily and hourly witnesses of the fidelity with which he painted both the scenes and the characters, amongst which the early part of his life was passed. I have often wondered how, with his intense love for the ocean, he could have lived so many years in an inland town. Occasionally though, he must have felt an uncontrollable desire to behold it, for his son records that he once mounted his horse and rode sixty miles to obtain a glimpse of it."

"But your own brother, Maude, appears to live happily away from it; though he, like yourself, spent all his early life on the coast."

"Yes, he is contented enough, I believe; but I often feel angry with him for not being miserable in London. Yet, as the greater portion of his time must be spent there, it is as well he should prefer 'the busy hum of men' to the roar of the mighty ocean. But I am often vexed with him for his insensibility on this account, though I am not the less proud of my brother; and shall be disappointed if you do not like him when he comes to fetch me in October, when, please to remember, you are to go with us to Baymouth."

"You are very kind to wish me to visit you, Maude; but I have never left my mother, and never intend doing so."

"Then why cannot Mrs. Travers come with you? My mother will be delighted to meet her again; and I am sure it will be better for both than moping here by yourselves. I will write to mamma this very day, and desire her to send the proper invitation directly. And do you, Nelly, induce your mother to accept it."

I endeavoured to dissuade Maude from writing to Mrs. Headley on such a subject. I knew my mother would refuse to leave home; and that if it was possible to get over that difficulty, the state of our finances would not warrant our incurring unnecessary expenses.

Maude laughed at all my excuses.

"I am never baffled, Nelly, when I have really set my heart on any project; and you will find yourself listening to the music of the waves before many weeks have blown over the head which has been shaking so wisely at all my persuasions for the last half-hour."

Maude's love for her only brother amounted almost to idolatry. She was never weary of talking of him, and had not, I believe, a thought in which he was not in some measure associated.

She kept, in compliance with his wish, a journal in which every event which occurred in her quiet life—and, I believe, nearly every feeling which arose in her heart—was recorded.

This was forwarded to him weekly in lieu of an ordinary letter, and he, in return, sent her long and amusing descriptions of the manner in which his own hours of relaxation were spent.

I could not, from my friend's account of her brother, form the least idea of his real character. Sometimes I was disposed to imagine he must be of a grave, retiring disposition, fond of solitude, and too much absorbed in contemplation to be either an agreeable or amiable companion; and at other times she would relate instances of his love of frolic and daring adventure, which it was difficult to associate with the character of a man devoted to a studious profession.

My mother and Mrs. Headley had been friends in girlhood, but owing to the distance which separated them when the latter married, the intimacy gradually failed, till nothing remained to remind them of it, except occasional friendly remembrances transmitted to each other through the medium of Mr. Lancester.

When the letter of invitation arrived, I was fully prepared for my mother's declining to accept it. She gave it to me with an expression of annoyance on her countenance.

"See, Nelly, how ungracious I must appear when I decline the affectionate entreaties of my old friend, Maude Lancester; but she little knows what an altered being she addresses. Her own life has passed so happily, that she cannot comprehend the wretchedness in which such a large portion of mine has been spent."

"But she, too, is a widow, mamma; and Maude has told me how greatly she suffered when her father was taken from them."

"One sorrow, Nelly, to counterbalance a host of blessings! Do you think I have not always been painfully conscious of the anxiety my own wretched state has occasioned all I have loved, that I have been a care and sorrow to all around me, and incapable of properly discharging the duties of wife or mother."

"And, dearest mother," interrupted I, eagerly, "loved all the more tenderly for the very reasons you deplore."

"I know it, Nelly. I was never insensible of the blessings I possessed in the love of husband and children; but think of my other causes of unhappiness—your sister's pitiable condition for so many years, and more than the loss of husband or the crippled state of my child—think of the tears of anguish I have shed; of the misery I still endure on account of your unhappy brother; and then you will not compare my lot, for a moment, with that of my old friend. I have had many sorrows to weep for, she but one.

"Mrs. Headley does not weep, mamma, Maude tells me; she is patiently resigned to God's will, and would consider it sinful to mourn as one without hope, because he she loved better than herself was chosen earlier for eternal felicity."

Greatly distressed at her evident unhappiness, I endeavoured to comfort her by reminding her that she had many blessings even now to be grateful for; that Esther's present happiness more than compensated for the pain and anxiety we had formerly suffered on her account.

"Besides, dearest mother," added I, "think of our dear Walter and Edmund, and of the comfort they will soon prove to you; and do not believe Mrs. Headley has more sources of happiness than yourself."

"That will do, dear. I am quite satisfied Mrs. Headley has no one who loves her more than my Nelly does her thankless mother. But will you answer this letter, and tell her how impossible it is for me to avail myself of her kindness."

Maude was greatly disappointed when told of my mother's decision, and accused me of not caring to visit her home.

"I tell you what it is, Nelly; your mother wants a companion to whom she can open her heart and obtain the sympathy she longs for. She will not do so to you for fear of saddening you. But I feel sure she has some ever-present grief on her heart, and each day she will find the weight of it become greater, unless she confides it to one capable of counselling her how to bear it. Since your father's death, it has only been some unusual excitement which has roused her to exertion of any kind — such as you told me your illness produced, and, in a minor degree, the preparations for Esther's marriage. She reminds me of the Alpine travellers I have read of, who, when overcome by the cold, would sink into heavy slumbers, from which they would never awaken if not violently aroused from the torpidity which steals over their faculties. She should be saved from mental death in the same rude manner, and you should devise some means by which it can effectually be done."

I pondered seriously over Maude's words, and could not but acknowledge their truth. I remembered how afraid I was to tell her of Henry's abstracting the money from the bank, and how the necessity for exertion dissipated the apathy which had followed my father's death.

Then I reflected on the words Mrs. Hurst had spoken to me concerning her.

"Your mother lives only in the past and future—the one she cannot think of without sorrow, the other without apprehension. We must get her to care for the present."

The hope of Esther's recovery had supplied this stimulus for the time, and when that was rendered certain, the preparations for her marriage occupied her mind for some time. But now, if Maude's surmises were correct —and she was insensibly, to me, falling back into the listless apathy from which my illness had roused her—what would become of us both?

But it was destined my fears should not be realised. A letter from Henry dispelled her anxiety and my secret apprehensions on his account. I could scarcely believe the evidence of my eyesight when it was placed in my hands. It was addressed to myself, but the envelope also contained a sealed letter for my mother.

It was dated from Montreal; and mine consisted only of a few lines very affectionately worded. Its purport was that as so long a time had elapsed since he had written home, he feared the sudden sight of his handwriting might agitate his mother, and, therefore, he had enclosed it to me that I might prepare her to receive it.

It is impossible to convey an idea of the conflicting feelings with which I perused this letter. Henry, in Canada, writing to me affectionately! No mention made of any visit to England since he had quitted it the previous year, gave me the certainty that the letter I had received from the hands of Jasper Coxe was a vile fabrication. Now, then, all my doubts were dissipated, and I might live in the blessed assurance that his power over me was ended. It was true Mr. Hurst had succeeded in convincing my reason on that point, but my fears were never silenced. I still could not, without a shudder of terror, pass the spot where that base woman had first accosted me.

I suppose my face must have betrayed to my mother I was the harbinger of joyful news, for, as I entered her room, she exclaimed—

"Nelly, have you heard from Esther again to-day? I do not know any other thing that could make you look so joyous!"

"No, dearest mother, my letter to-day is more welcome than even one from my sister!"

I laid a slight stress on the word sister; and my mother, starting from her seat, cried—

"It is from Henry! It is from my son! Oh! quick, quick, Nelly! let me see the proof that he is still living!"

I first put into her hands the few lines addressed to me, and when she had read them, gave her the letter to herself. Before breaking the seal, she pressed it to her lips, and, bursting into tears, said—

"Leave me, my dear, for a time—I must thank God for this great mercy, before I gladden my eyes with the words addressed to me by my child!"

I hastened to tell Martha the joyful news of Henry's safety and absence from England; and her heart, like my own, was lightened of a heavy burthen by the intelligence I imparted.

When recalled by my mother, she was still weeping; but seeing my look of distress, she said—

"Do not look so grieved, Nelly: these are tears of joy and gratitude. Read your brother's letter, and see if I have not reason to shed them. God has hearkened to my prayers, and preserved my son from sin and from danger!"

The letter was long and affectionate. He spoke hopefully of his present condition; but expressed his regret that his past errors necessitated a banishment from home and country.

His prospects, he stated, were encouraging for the future. He had been received as junior partner in a mercantile house at Montreal, but without mentioning the firm to which he was allied. He had delayed writing till he could send satisfactory accounts of his proceedings; and now that his position was assured, he had not lost an hour in imparting the welcome intelligence to his mother.

The conclusion of his letter rather staggered my belief in his prosperity.

"A confidential agent in our house is on the point of sailing for England; business transactions with a large house in Liverpool will detain him there for a short time, and he will bring me letters from home. As it was a condition, when admitted a partner in this firm, that I should place five hundred pounds more in the business, I ventured to agree to such a stipulation, sure, my dearest mother, that you would enable me to keep my word, by assisting me with the necessary amount. Our agent will take charge of the money in the letter you address to me, if you will transmit it to him.

"His address will be, Mr. Onias Heath, care of Messrs. Staples, Ship-agents, Liverpool."

"Well, Nelly," said my mother, as I returned her the letter, while her face looked radiant with happiness, "is not this enough to rejoice our hearts, and render us thankful to God? I will tell you now what you would never had known had we not received these glad tidings of my poor boy, that for months past I have felt agonising remorse for allowing him to leave England unaccompanied by myself. I have felt how criminal it was to launch in a new world, and in a new career, one so little capable of self-guidance; and I am blessed far above my deserts for such a desertion of a mother's duties!"

That my mother could, even in a wild dream, have thought of leaving Esther and myself, to follow the uncertain career which the vices of Henry had compelled him to adopt, was such an astounding thing, that I could only gaze at her in speechless surprise and consternation!

"Don't look so bewildered, Nelly, at my words, or imagine from them that I love your brother above my other children. But is it not a mother's part to give her greatest care to the one who stands in greatest need of it? And was not Henry the most helpless of mine, in his inability to resist temptation to evil; was it not likely to assail him, when thrown, without a friend to guide him among strangers, in a strange land? But now my fears on his account are at rest for ever! If safe for one year, and that the most perilous, from his being without friends or employment, surely we may trust him for the future. Read the letter once more, dear! I did not observe the day he mentioned for the money to reach Liverpool."

It was to be there on the twentieth of that month. It was now the fifteenth. Surely the agent would not have come to England for a few days only!

"What is the date of the letter?" asked my mother.

I looked. It was August the eleventh. Esther's wedding-day!

"A happy omen, if we needed one, for her happiness, Nelly!"

"But still, mamma, I cannot understand why we did not receive this letter earlier."

"Mr. Heath, in the multiplicity of his business, must have forgotten to post it, dear. But we have no time to lose. I must start with Martha for London, to-morrow, and procure this money. I can leave you with Maude, without fear of your being lonely. And,

Nelly," continued she, in a hesitating voice, as if she was about to say what she felt I should object to, "I should like to proceed to Liverpool, and myself deliver it into the custody of this person. What an addition to my happiness it will be to converse with one who not long since was in the society of my son!"

"Dear mamma," answered I, "pray allow me to go with you instead of Martha. You have been out so little lately—are so unfitted for exertion—that I fear you will not prove equal to the fatigue."

"The more reason for Martha's services, then, Nelly, she will be a better prop to me than you can be; but you surely remember the words of your favourite poet, 'A merry heart goes all the way, a sad one tires in a mile.' But the first step in this journey must be taken to-night; write to Mr. Stockdale, and acquaint him with my immediate necessity for five hundred pounds."

The mention of that man's name brought back to my recollection the conversation I had held with Mr. Lancester on the morning of his departure. I had been expecting to hear from him on the subject, and in compliance with his advice waited till I did so, before informing my mother of the heavy loss she had sustained by her agent's failure. Now it was imperative I should do so directly. Still, however, reluctant to do it abruptly, I inquired whether it would not be more advisable to write and direct Mr. Bingley to procure the money.

"No, Nelly," was the reply; "I do not like Mr. Bingley. The truth is, dear," she added, "he presumes too much on his knowledge of my affairs, and thinks, because your father reposed much confidence in his judgment, he is authorised to dictate to me on subjects of which I alone am competent to decide. Besides, it would only entail additional expense, as he cannot dispense with the assistance of a stockbroker more than myself."

I had then to break to her the intelligence of the heavy loss she had sustained through her misplaced confidence in the person she had formerly employed. Perhaps, if I had been compelled to acquaint her with it the previous day, it might have affected her differently; as it was, her heart was so completely filled with joy at the receipt of Henry's letter, that I do not think she would have experienced a moment's uneasiness had the loss been of double the amount.

"This is very unfortunate," she replied, tranquilly, when I had finished my story, "the more particularly as I dislike applying to Mr. Bingley, and yet should object to employ a total stranger to procure this money."

"Let me write to Mr. Lancester, then, mamma, and tell him you will be in town to-morrow, and wish him to call on you as soon as possible after your arrival."

To this my mother willingly consented, and when I had finished my letter I walked to the Vicarage for the purpose of communicating my good news to my friends there, by whom it was received with delight almost equal to my own.

Mr. Hurst could not, however, refrain from triumphing a little in his own penetration.

"Did I not tell you, Nelly, that you would hear no more from your tormentors, that they knew the game was up from the moment you confided their persecutions to those who were sure to detect the falsehoods they had invented for the purpose of playing on your fears. I think I am not doing my duty as a friend if I do not endeavour to discover them, and have them punished for the infamous manner in which they extorted those sums of money from you."

"Pray do not, Mr. Hurst!" said I. "That money was given to keep secret from my mother what I thought it would kill her to become acquainted with, and of which I would willingly she should for ever remain in ignorance, no matter at what amount of suffering to myself."

"Well, Nelly, let the past rest in oblivion, but any further attempts on your tranquillity and purse I must insist on resenting in my own way."

CHAPTER XVI.

The next morning, my mother, resisting all my entreaties for permission to accompany her, departed with Martha for London. I had endeavoured in vain to persuade her not to visit Liverpool. I was certain such a long and hurried journey would prove injurious to her, but she was firm in her determination to deliver the money herself into the hands of my brother's agent.

"I shall not be assured he receives it safely, Nelly, unless I go. The time is so short, owing to his neglect in forwarding your brother's letter, that he may possibly leave Liverpool before the letter could reach him; I shall be able to do so as soon as the post, and thus be certain it will not be lost."

My dear mother was, I believe, quite unconscious that she was in reality very happy the negligence of Mr. Heath in forwarding Henry's letter gave her, as she considered, a legitimate excuse for seeking an interview with one who had recently parted from her son, and thus enable her to gain more information respecting him than his own letter afforded. Her face was again bright with intelligence and joy—new life and strength appeared to animate her frame. As she embraced me for the last time, she said, gaily,

"Don't weep, Nelly, that I am leaving you for a few days; think only of the happiness we shall both feel when I return to you, still more assured of Henry's health and prosperity. I feel that the gloom which occasionally steals over my heart has departed for ever. You will not only welcome back your mother, but your friend and companion. Take care of my Nelly, Maude, and do not suffer her to be apprehensive on my account; I could travel safely through the world under the charge of such a faithful guardian as this." She placed her hand on Martha's shoulder as she spoke, who looked nearly as happy as her mistress.

"Come, Nelly," cried Maude, when I could no longer discern the train which carried my mother away, "let us return home at once. I am appointed your custodian during your mother's absence, and I intend to prove a very arbitrary one; you have nothing to look so dismal about, the excitement of the journey will prove of the greatest service to Mrs. Travers. Indeed, it seems incredible to me that the bright face we have just lost sight of, is the same woe-begone one I looked on two days ago. If she was my mother, I would take care she should never fall back into the condition from which she has just awakened."

"How would you prevent it, Maude? You have seen how gradually the shadow has crept over her since Esther left us."

"You have tried no means, Nelly, to check the malady. You should have insisted on her leaving this place directly after your sister's wedding; new ideas must displace old ones, however rooted they may be in the mind.

It is the constant brooding over one particular evil which frequently leads to the commission of suicide. Many may, perhaps, have been saved from perpetrating that dreadful crime, by a greater calamity befalling them than the one they have suffered to engross all their thoughts, and which they were willing to face death rather than endure. Even personal discomforts, and those of the most petty kind, will often prove serviceable to a 'mind diseased.' There are few cases in which mental pain does not yield to physical. When I see anyone looking particularly miserable, I always wish they could have a good strong fit of toothache; it would do them a great deal of good in a moral point of view."

"Thank God! Maude, there will be no fear for the future. Once convinced of Henry's safety and well doing, she will have no painful subjects on which to meditate."

"If you think that, Nelly, you have profited very little by experience. One so accustomed as your mother to feel apprehension for a beloved object, will not easily believe there is no longer cause for anxiety."

"But if we hear frequently from Henry, as he has promised we shall," said I, "there will really be no ground for uneasiness."

"Very true, *if* you do, Nelly; but you have told me he never has been a good correspondent, and his silence will infallibly be interpreted by your mother as a proof of misfortune having overtaken him. The only thing *good* that could happen to her," continued my lively friend, "would be *evil*—paradoxical, but true. I wish something very disagreeable would happen to you, Nelly, such as we read of in novels—your banker run off with your money, or a fire destroy your most valuable property the very day your insurance had expired, or your lawyer discover that the sum you had lent on mortgage was all lost in consequence of a flaw in the title-deeds. Of course, under such circumstances, you would be too high-minded to receive assistance from your friends, and you would consent to live in the old haunted house at Baymouth, where two rooms would be made habitable for you; and you would make beautiful drawings of the beautiful views in the neighbourhood, and I would send them to London, and Cuthbert should dispose of them to some enthusiastic amateur, and your mother would be too solicitous for the health and welfare of the child who was working for her daily bread, to brood over the imaginary ills of the one who was absent; and then, by and by, when you are at the lowest ebb of your fortunes, the tide should turn; the banker, or the lawyer, or the insurance people, will pay back all the money, and the story end with my standing as bridesmaid while you are going through the delightful ceremony of matrimony with the enthusiastic amateur, who must prove an earl at the very least."

I laughed heartily at the lively romance Maude had constructed for my benefit, and yet it awakened unpleasant reflections.

"I don't know, Maude," I answered, "that I shall ever require your brother to walk about London with a portfolio of my drawings under his arm, but perhaps we may soon be glad to find a cheaper home than this, and if we are compelled to quit it, I will commission you to fit up the rooms in the haunted house you talk of, and where I suppose I am to make the acquaintance of the noble earl you have so generously bestowed on me. It would be some consolation during our temporary distress, to reside near yourself."

"You had better, then, go with me when I return, and make acquaintance with your future domicile. You will not only reside near us, but under the same roof, for we have some of the rooms in this same haunted house; there are plenty left, though, for you, on the opposite side."

The next morning brought me a letter from Martha. They had arrived safely at Streatham, where, thanks to Susan's good management, all was ready for their reception. My mother was too much fatigued to write herself, but would do so the following day.

"What a blessing it is, my dear Miss Nelly," wrote my faithful nurse, "that I have left you without fear of your being troubled by that bad man and woman; had my mis tress known and suffered through their vile falsehoods as you have done, she would never have lived to see this happy day. Mr. Lancester has just left her; he wished her to go to his house while she remained in town, as he thought it might be painful to be here alone, but she told him she was too grateful to God for His present mercies to suffer herself to feel unhappy by the recollections of past sorrows. She has not said positively she will go to Liverpool to-morrow, but I do not doubt she intends doing so."

The following morning brought me the eagerly expected letter from my mother. She had obtained the money through the agency of Mr. Bingley, but evidently deeply resented his remonstrances on the subject.

"He tells me, Nelly, that I ought to spend only four, or, at the most, five hundred a year, instead of eight. I am content to do so. Your father left to me every shilling he died possessed of, but it was for the benefit of his children he reposed such confidence in their mother; it is only for their sakes I value the money. Is it not better I should have the delight of seeing them happy and prosperous, than suffer them to wait for my death to benefit by that I only hold in trust for them? I start to-morrow for Liverpool, and will write to you from thence. You need not be apprehensive I shall suffer from fatigue, Martha will not allow me to exert myself more than she considers prudent."

Satisfied that my mother was well and happy, and that she would return to me in a few days, I, for the first time since she had been with me, really enjoyed the gay companionship of my friend. We, at the earnest request of Mrs. Hurst, passed the greater portion of our time at the Vicarage, where Maude became an especial favourite with its master. For her amusement the cosmorama was lighted of an evening, and she delighted the heart of the artist by the genuine admiration she expressed for its glories.

To my great delight, I could now look at the beautiful Jezebel without shuddering; she, of whom it reminded me, was nothing but a memory, painful as regarded the past, but unfeared for the future.

"Have you been to Wishart's farm, lately?" asked Mr. Hurst, as he placed the picture for Maude's inspection. I replied in the negative.

"Then I wish you would do so to-morrow; he is very ill, and his poor daughter is nearly worn out with fatigue and anxiety. Nothing appears to give her so much pleasure as your visits, and the old man is less impatient when you are present than he is with any other visitant."

I had not lately been a frequent visitor to the cottage of the old farmer. I was fearful of raising his captious temper by taking Maude with me, and I now told Mr. Hurst he must take her for a long ride on the morrow, if I was not to be her companion in the morning.

As I became better acquainted with Mrs. Locksley, I learned to value her character highly. Her one great grief appeared ever present in her heart, but it did not, as it would in some natures, have closed it against the sorrows of others. She bore her heavy cross with humble submission to God's will; her quiet and resigned demeanor, the kindness and benevolence she was constantly exercising towards those around her who needed assistance, in any shape she could alleviate, the affectionate solicitude with which she attended on her father, and the gentle submission with which she bore his occasional savage outbursts of temper, whenever she firmly, but respectfully, resisted his attempts to overreach those with whom he had pecuniary dealings, caused me to regard her with feelings of almost affectionate reverence, and I used to think the fervent prayers of such a righteous person for her daughter's reformation would avail much in the sight of God, and that in His own good time they would be answered.

Whenever I had lately visited the farm, I had reached it by a circuitous route; but on the morning following Mr. Hurst's request that I would go there, I boldly ventured by the way where I had been accosted by the woman Rachel.

I found Mrs. Locksley looking more unwell and depressed than usual, but her face lighted up as I approached, and she warmly thanked me for my goodness, as she styled it, in coming to see her.

I told her, with truth, that it gave me pleasure to do so, and that I would become a more frequent visitor. I then inquired after her father.

"He is better to-day," she answered.

The voice was so sad that uttered the words, that had I not been well acquainted with the love and duty she always showed towards her arbitrary parent, I should have imagined his amendment a subject of regret instead of satisfaction.

As if in answer to my thoughts, she said—

"I am thankful he is well enough to leave his room; but, dear young lady, do not condemn me for seeming sad when I ought only to rejoice. My father will, I hope and believe, be restored to health; but, unfortunately, his old feelings and prejudices seem stronger rooted than ever; and I had so hoped the sufferings he had passed through, would have softened his heart, and weakened in it the love of money, which has lately become such a fatal passion."

At this moment his voice was heard impatiently calling his daughter.

"Who beest thee maundering with, Hannah? It's some sneaking body, I'll be bound, who has come to beg of us! Send 'em away, I say—or I'll manage to come out and pay into 'em with my stick! Come here to me directly, and let me hear who 't is."

Mrs. Locksley, with a frightened look, was preparing to obey his summons, when I whispered, "Let me go in alone to see him."

I entered the kitchen, while the old man was still storming with rage. He was seated in his customary three-cornered walnut-wood arm-chair, which was placed some little distance up the wide, old-fashioned chimney, where a large wood fire was blazing.

He did not recognise me directly, but still perceived it was not his daughter who advanced towards him.

"Ha!" cried he, as he attempted to rise from the chair, while he brandished his stick, "you have got the boldness to come in, have you? But be off, or you'll rue it pretty quick, I tell 'ee!"

"Do you not know me, Master Wishart?" said I, holding out my hand as I spoke.

"Is it only you?" replied he, looking a little ashamed, and sinking back in his chair. "I thought Hannah was giving victuals away to some of the beggars that come canting round her when I am out of the way. I'll soon clear the place of 'em though, the lazy varment!"

"I am glad to see you so much better, farmer," said I, when he would allow me to speak.

"Oh, yes!" was the reply, in a fretful voice, "I 'spose I am better, but I want to be well! What's the use of a fellow's sitting here all day, when he wants to be about his farm? I can 'tend to business a bit though, now—so if you wants chickens, you must give me five shillings a couple for them, or you won't get 'em from me! Tell me how many you want, and then you can pay me before Hannah comes in, and you needn't say anything to her about the price."

Though I had not intended purchasing any when I entered, I readily agreed to humour him, and thus ensure his good humour during the time I remained.

We had just settled our bargain, and the money carefully deposited in the large canvass bag he always carried in the pocket of his coat, when his daughter entered with a basin of broth for the invalid.

"This is how she serves me," said he, in a piteous voice, as she placed it on the small round table by his side. " Nothing but spoon meat will she give me, and how is a poor old fellow to get strong on such watery stuff as this? Do let me have a tankard of ale and a rasher, there's a good wench; and then thy old father will soon be in the fields again."

"In a day or two, father. But you know the doctor said you must be careful for a time."

"Oh! that's the way she rules me," said he, with a grim smile. "Wait a bit, my lass, and I'll show you who's master here once more!

"Now, don't you go!" cried he, as I rose to depart; "stay whiles I drink this slop—I wants to have some talk with 'ee."

During the time he was swallowing the despised broth, I occupied myself by looking, with admiring eyes, round the kitchen; which, thanks to Mrs. Locksley's labour, was as bright and pleasant an apartment as the eye could wish to rest on.

It was a large, low room, with an immense fireplace, in which there were usually two long settles; one of these had been removed, in order that the old man's favourite chair might occupy its place. The floor was of bricks, laid as evenly as the smoothest boards; and, from the rubbing they constantly received, were both bright and dry. Against the wall, facing the wide, low casement window, was placed a large dresser; the top shelves of which were garnished with great round dishes of pewter, while lower down were rows of plates of the same metal.

No silver could be brighter than these appeared, as the sun's rays danced and glittered through the narrow panes of the lattice.

A huge, old-fashioned clock ticked loudly in a large, black, polished case, in one corner of the room. This clock was the pride of the old farmer's heart; it had belonged to several generations of Wisharts before it had descended to himself. It was a wonderful clock, the old man used to tell his admiring friends. It not only marked correctly the hour of the day, but likewise accurately recorded on its dial the days of the months and weeks, with the age of the moon, and the hours for its rising and setting.

Over the high, quaintly-carved chimney-piece, was a long, narrow, looking-glass, in a black frame—tilted very forward from the wall; whilst in the top of the frame were stuck several tall feathers from the tail of the peacock, which waved solemnly to and fro whenever a sudden draught of air entered the room.

In the corner opposite the clock, was an equally cherished article of bygone days. It was a large three-cornered beaufet, with glass doors, through which the eyes of a connoisseur would have gazed delighted on the rare old china bowls and plates, mixed with a variety of other articles equally valuable to a collector of such curiosities. There were little cups, without handles, placed in saucers equally tiny; and of which the china was so exquisitely transparent, that I could see through them as they stood in all their glory in front of the larger articles.

Then there were tea-pots to match these fairy cups, some of which were furnished with silver spouts; but whether they were imported in that state from the Celestial Empire, or whether they had replaced others of more fragile material, I was unable to learn from their present possessor, who remembered them in his grandfather's time having the same metallic noses.

Another corner of the room was occupied by a similar cupboard to that which contained the china, and its contents were still more highly prized by the old man. It was filled with a beautiful collection of the British birds' eggs, formed by himself when a youth, and would have driven many an admirer of such ornithological curiosities mad with envy. They were arranged on shelves, each specimen reposing on a slip of paper, on which its name was written in a beautifully clear hand. From the tiny egg of the tomtit, up to that of the royal eagle, not one was missing in the link.

"Ah!" would the owner of these treasures say, when they called forth the admiration of the spectator, "I never took so much trouble about anything in my life, as I did to get them eggs. I used to tease every body that came anigh the place to help me in finding those I could not get in these parts; and as I used to go with father to the large cattle fairs all over the country, I had a better chance than most lads of finding what I wanted.

"I thought when I married, and got that thing to put 'em in, and paid old Jarvis, the clerk, to write all the names for 'em, how proud I should be to show 'em a boy of my own, and tell him of the fun I had in getting some of 'em, and the trouble t'others cost me, and how I nearly broke my neck in getting a raven's nest, when the large branch of the tree broke, and I fell, eggs and all, to the ground—every one of 'em smashed, but the one there!

"But there, I never had a son or a grandson either; and when I am dead and gone, I dare say they will be thrown away as rubbish."

And the old man would sigh heavily at this sad thought, and cast a look of troubled affection towards the cherished memorial of his youthful days.

Besides all the treasures I have mentioned, the ample room contained many more household gods. There was a large high chest of drawers, made of walnut-wood, with long brass handles, and on the top of this were shelves enclosed by panelled doors. This antique piece of furniture stood by the side of the window, and was so highly polished by what old-fashioned housewives call "elbow-grease," that it reflected, like a looking-glass, all that passed before it.

On these shelves was deposited the large old family Bible, with brass fastenings, in which the births, marriages, and deaths of many generations of Wisharts were duly recorded. But the Bible was not the only volume carefully preserved in this old-fashioned bookcase. There was the "Pilgrim's Progress," illustrated by the most horrible pictures of the dangers which attended the journey of the brave Christian; and the leaves of which were nearly as brown with age, as was the leather in which they were bound.

The original collector of farmer Wishart's library must have possessed rather a diversified taste for literature; for, in addition to "Foxe's Book of Martyrs," "Robinson Crusoe," "The History of the Great Plague," "The Works of Bishop Burnett," and "Commodore Anson's Voyage Round the World," there was a well-thumbed copy of a work, in several large volumes, filled with an account of the wars of the Duke of Marlborough and Prince Eugene.

The very walls of that well-plenished kitchen were adorned with wealth in the shape of foxes' brushes, stuffed badgers, a tremendous pair of polished horns, which had once belonged to an ox, for which the farmer had obtained a prize at some county agriculture exhibition; while several old-fashioned guns, with single barrels and flint locks, but kept bright with incessant care, glittered against the oaken panels. These were treasures their owner would not have exchanged for the best double-barrelled and percussion guns that ever left the manufactories of Egg or Joe Manton.

While I was taking this mental inventory of the farmer's kitchen, I was startled by his pushing from him, with violence, the table on which his daughter had placed his basin of broth.

"You may well look!" cried he, as I hastily withdrew my eyes from the polished doors of the walnut-wood press opposite which I was seated. "You won't find many small farmers with better things about them than George Wishart. Ain't it enough!' he continued vehemently, "to make a man fight a hard battle with death? when, for what he knows, he'll hardly be laid in his grave, before the very bed he dies on will be canted out of his house! Why don't Hannah let her girl come home—for all that's come and gone—

there's many a man would make her a good husband for the sake of old Wishart's savings?"

"Has Mrs. Locksley heard from her daughter? Does she wish to return home?" inquired I, eagerly.

"Not likely she should, poor lass! The last time she was here her mother did nought but cry and whine over her. 'Tain't likely, a girl of spirit—and Hannah always had plenty of that—would stand being preached to all day!"

At this moment, Mrs. Locksley entered the room, and, anxious she should not hear her father speak of her unfortunate daughter, I prepared to depart; but he had worked himself into a rage, and could not be prevented from hurling some of it at the poor woman.

"I have been telling the young madam what an unnatural mother you have been all your life! When your daughter came home, you drove her away again by your doing all you could to make her miserable. You are fond enough of reading the Bible to me; and the other day, when I was too ill to argy with 'ee, you read the chapter about the prodigal son. I wondered, at the time, you weren't ashamed to hear the words as they came out of your mouth. Was that the way you welcomed Hannah home?"

"The prodigal, in the parable, returned repentant, father; Hannah came to us while still living in her sin! But go, young lady—pray leave us! These are no words for your ears. Father will be sorry he has spoken them by and by."

I left the farm more than ever grieved for the unhappy mother; but not before the old man had made me promise to visit him again quickly.

CHAPTER XVII.

The letter I received from my mother, the day following her arrival at Liverpool, contained nothing but satisfactory intelligence; foremost amongst which, was the announcement of her own probable return on the day following my receipt of her letter.

She had seen Mr. Heath, although she had had considerable trouble in obtaining an interview with him; and did not seem very favourably impressed with his appearance and manner, when she succeeded in doing so.

"He is not the kind of person I expected to see, Nelly, and think most probably he left this country in a very different position to the one he now occupies; but he spoke very highly of your brother, and of the estimation in which he was held by his employers. It is certain he must be a most trustworthy person, or he would not have been sent to England for the purpose of investing a large sum of money in the purchase of Birmingham and Manchester manufactures. It was owing to his being engaged in seeing them safely shipped that I had to wait some time before I could see him.

"Think, dear, with what delight I heard him speak of the likelihood of Henry's being in England next Spring, to transact business of a similar character in lieu of himself."

I was not disappointed respecting my mother's return at the time she had fixed. She looked pale and languid, but declared she felt perfectly well; and, in answer to my anxious inquiries, said she only required rest to recruit her.

"Joy and sorrow are equally enemies to sleep, my child. I have been too happy since I received Henry's letter to discern how much I stood in need of it. Now that I have discharged my duty, I feel that I have earned repose. I should not have felt I had acted rightly, had I not seen the agent he had commissioned to receive the money."

"But you did not appear to like him much, mamma!"

"I did not, dear; and sincerely hope he has not much intercourse with your brother; although, I own, he appeared intimately acquainted with him. I suppose, as the junior partner, Henry has to transact business with those employed confidentially by the firm."

"But what business is it he is engaged in?" I inquired. "He did not mention it in his letter, or the names of the gentlemen who conduct it."

"Unfortunately, Nelly," said my mother, with a look of vexation, "I neglected to ask such very necessary questions. I fully intended doing so, but Mr. Heath was in such haste to return to the docks, and the short time we were together was so wholly occupied by my inquiries respecting Henry's health and welfare, that I never even thought of obtaining his correct address; and after my letter was sealed, I remembered so many things I wished to say, that I intended writing to him again immediately. Now I must wait for his next letter before I can do so."

My mother was unable to leave her room for several days after her return home. The excitement which had given her the power of undergoing such fatigue was gone, and she suffered violently from the reaction. Rest and quietness were the only remedies for her recovery, and, assured of this, I passed the time happily with Maude—the only drawback to my enjoyment being her approaching departure.

"I don't know what I shall do without you, Maude," said I, one afternoon, when we were returning from a long ramble, "I shall never care to walk when you are gone."

"You will get used to it in time," answered she, carelessly. "I ought to have been home a week ago, and then Cuthbert would have come for me; and although my mother does not say so in her letters, I am sure she wishes me to return. I did not like to leave you while Mrs. Travers was so unwell, but now she is recovered sufficiently to come down stairs, I shall take my departure at once. I have written home to say I shall be there the day after to-morrow."

I felt greatly hurt at the indifferent manner in which Maude spoke of our approaching separation. I had learned to regard her with so much affection—to find such pleasure in her society—that I was both pained and indignant at her evident wish to quit me. Endeavouring, as much as possible, to conceal the annoyance I really felt, I answered coldly, "That I was sorry her good-nature had induced her to remain longer at Brookfields than suited her convenience."

"Don't say anything about that," was the reply to my rather rude remark. "I have been very happy during the time I have been here, and shall hope to visit you again; but I cannot say I am sorry at the prospect of returning home. I assure you, Nelly, you will not miss me as much as you imagine."

"You judge me by your own feelings, Maude."

"Of course I do. You have known me long enough, Nelly, to know I do not possess a grain of what is called 'sentiment.' 'I should be a fool to weep at what I am glad of.' Now don't look so grieved at what you think my unkindness. You will forgive me, I hope, before we really do shake hands and part. But, look!" she continued, as she approached a window where my mother was seated, " there is Mrs. Travers actually waiting dinner for us! Won't Martha scold us for being so late!"

Maude was very lively and talkative during the meal, and several times endeavoured to draw me into the conversation, but I somewhat sullenly repulsed her attempts to do so, and secretly accused her of hypocrisy when she addressed me affectionately.

My mother, on the contrary, appeared amused and interested by her young visitor's cheerfulness; and, finding my silence seemed unnoticed or uncared for by either, I quitted them, and, in the solitude of my own room, indulged, without restraint, in the grief I had with difficulty suppressed the whole day, at the evident want of affection which Maude's conduct manifested for me.

After a time, sorrow gave place to anger,

and I hastily commenced collecting together many little memorials of our friendship I had received from her. While thus employed, I was startled by her sudden appearance.

"What are you moping up here for?" cried she gaily, as she entered. "Mamma and I have been so busy settling our plans, that we did not miss you till this minute, and now I am come to tell you what they are."

I answered, with what I considered quiet dignity, "I do not care to know them; but I am glad you are here, for it gives me the opportunity of returning to you these things. I cannot consent to retain them, since it is evident you no longer regard me with affection. In the words of Ophelia, I say:

'Rich gifts wax poor, when givers prove unkind!'"

To my inexpressible mortification, I could perceive Maude had some difficulty to prevent herself from laughing. She, however, controlled the inclination, and, looking at the articles spread on the table, said, with mock gravity—

"You are pleased to be satirical, Nelly; the 'rich gifts,' as you term them, are certainly too poor to be worth your preserving. But you might have waited till I had left you, and then made a bonfire of them if you liked. I have seen all day that you have been longing to quarrel with me, but I did not choose to indulge such an unamiable propensity, and am come for the purpose of setting you an example of returning good for evil, by assisting you to get ready for your journey."

My look of astonishment must, I suppose, have been very ridiculous; for Maude, no longer able to restrain herself, laughed merrily for some moments, and then throwing her arms round my neck, and kissing me affectionately, said—

"Oh, Nelly, Nelly! you must have very unkind thoughts towards your friends, or you would not imagine they cared so little for yourself. You have favoured me with a quotation, I will give you one much more to the purpose:

> 'By the pattern of my own thoughts,
> I cut out the purity of his.'

But I have just achieved such a triumph over your mother's prejudices that I can afford to be merciful to your's. She has consented to accept the pressing invitation which my mother enclosed in the letter I received this morning; and it was because I determined she should do so, that I did not weep and lament over our approaching separation. Now will you have the goodness to put these 'rich gifts' into your drawers again, and remember, for the future, there are people in the world as capable of feeling affection as yourself."

"Oh, Maude!" said I, incredulously, when her homily concluded, she stood waiting for my reply. "It is not possible my mother will go to Baymouth; when I urged her to do so, she most positively refused."

"You need not be jealous of my superior influence, Nelly; you went the wrong way to work, and entreated her to leave home for her own sake. I urged her to do so for your's."

"Then you did very wrong," said I, angrily. "I will not suffer her to think I am selfish enough to take such a mean advantage of her love for me. How could you be so cruel towards us both?"

"Listen to me!" said my friend, as I was about to hasten to my mother. "If your mother were ill, would you not prevail on her to adopt the remedies you considered necessary for her recovery? Would you not implore her to do so for your sake? And now that she has consented to take the medicine, which will preserve her in health, you turn indignantly round on the physician who has persuaded her to swallow it. Forgive me, Nelly, if I have appeared unkind, but you will be the better for the lesson I hope, and not distrust your friends whenever they may act in a way you do not, for the time, comprehend. I could not feign sorrow at parting from you when I believed it would only be for a day or two; and I did not wish you to know of my intention of appealing to your mother's affection for you, for the purpose of benefitting herself. Now go to her, if you please—you will find I have done no harm by my interference."

"Not till I have obtained your forgiveness," said I, humbly.

"You need not wait long for that, dear. There, that will do! Now dry your eyes like a good child, or mamma will think I have been telling stories, and that you don't wish to visit Baymouth."

Despite the reasoning of Maude, I could not but regret my mother's consent to leave home was obtained by the representation that to do so would prove beneficial to myself, and felt as guilty when I met her as if I was in reality the selfish being I dreaded she would consider me. Her first words, however, convinced me that my friend had done her "spiriting gently."

"My dear Nelly, Maude has given me a note from her mother, and the invitation it contains is such a very kind and pressing one, that if you do not object we will accept it, and follow her to Baymouth as soon as we can manage to leave home. You see," added she, cheerfully, "that my visit to Liverpool is already producing good results; for it has given me the confidence requisite to mix with strangers once more."

"But Mrs. Headley is no stranger, mamma. You have told me you were fast friends once on a time."

"True, dear; but that once on a time is a long while ago, and I fear it will prove as difficult to resuscitate an old friendship as to form a new one. More painful, I feel, it will prove to both."

"Then why endeavour to do so, mamma? Why not decline this invitation as you did the former one?"

"Have you never heard that second thoughts are best, Nelly? Besides, it was more difficult to resist Maude's arguments than your own; and she did not cease to press them, till I had written a few lines to her mother, conveying my acceptance of her proffered kindness. So now there is nothing to be done but prepare to follow her as quickly as we can."

I was not wise enough, or old enough, to regard my first visit from home as a commonplace event. I could think of nothing after

Maude's departure, but of the pleasure I should feel in rejoining her at Baymouth. To be sure, I had an unpleasant consiousness that I had been the scapegoat which had induced my mother to consent to enter the wilderness of the world she had quitted for many years. But Mrs. Hurst laughed at my scruples on such a point.

"You will come back wiser and better than you leave it, dear," said my kind friend. "A month's absence, even from the happiest home, is of service to the mind. You will receive new ideas every mile you travel; the mental vision delights in 'fresh fields and pastures new' as much as the physical. Your mother furnishes a striking illustration of this truism. Therefore, Nelly, do not expect me to condole with you on what I am sure will prove of great service to you."

I had to take leave of many of my village friends after I quitted the Vicarage; amongst others, of Mrs. Locksley.

When I reached the farm, I found her, as usual, actively employed; but with a troubled, saddened look, very different to her usual one of patient resignation.

In answer to my inquiry for her father, she said, with a voice quivering with emotion—

"I wish I could say he was better; but day after day goes by, and he is still unable to leave his chair by the fire, and each day he becomes more impatient of the confinement and harsher to those who have occasion to seek him on matters of business, he will not allow me to transact for him. He thinks that I shall sell the old place and furniture when he is dead, and that thought troubles him night and day. He has threatened to make a will, leaving everything from me; and accuses me of driving from the place one for whose welfare I would willingly lay down my own life. But he will be glad to see you," said the poor woman, wiping the tears from her face, "if you will go in to him."

I found the farmer looking much as he had done a few days previously. To my surprise, he was occupied in writing on the small table which usually was placed by his side in the ample chimney. But he laid down the pen as I entered, and eagerly welcomed me. Then turning to his daughter, he said—

"I wish, Hannah, you would go down to Standen's, and get me a new pen. Young madam will stay with me while you are gone, won't 'ee?"

The last word was addressed to me, and I willingly consented to remain with him till his daughter returned from the village.

The farmer watched her from the window as long as she remained in view, and, then turning to me with a look of relief, said—

"Now she's gone, I can say what I want to you. Will you write on this paper for me what I have been trying to do all the morning? For I be but a poor hand with the pen—schollards weren't in fashion when I was a youngster!"

"Certainly," I answered; "but your daughter would have helped you quite as well as I can."

"Yes; she, maybe, would have done it for me, but what would have been the good of

,it; she wouldn't have put it in post when 'twas done. Now, look, young madam, I wants you to finish this as I tells ye," and he held towards me the paper on which he had written a few words. "Read it out, will 'ee?" said he, impatiently, and I did as he required.

"'Twenty pounds reward.—This is to give notis, that I, George Wishart, of Sandhill Farm, will give twenty pounds......'"

"That's all I can manage," said the old man, when I had read the lines. "Now I want you to finish it for me, and send it to the people in Lunnon, who will put it in the papers. Sit down, will 'ee, and write what I'll tell 'ee. Let's see, what's the last words? 'I, George Wishart, will give twenty pounds' —yes, that's right. Now, then, go on as fast as ye can—will give twenty pounds to anybody who will find Hannah Locksley, and tell her that her old grandfather's very bad, and wants to see her before he dies. That's all," said he, when I had written the words he dictated; "now fold it up and seal it, and direct it to the people in Lunnon. who will put it in the papers. Stay, it will cost money,

I s'pose," and taking the well-filled canvass bag from his pocket he extended a sovereign towards me.

"But, Mr. Wishart," said I, "this advertisement will not cost so much money as that. Had you not better let your daughter take it to the post-office, and get Mr. Standen to manage it for her?"

"No!" cried the old man, vehemently; "Hannah don't want the poor lass home. She won't have it put in the papers if she knows aught of it. Now do, there's a dear young madam, put it in the post yourself; just wrop the money inside the letter, and tell 'em to spend it all in finding her. I can't die easy if I don't see the poor girl again; I beant unnatural to my own flesh and blood if other folk be."

Very reluctantly I enclosed the sovereign in the paper; the old man then, with trembling eagerness, watched me fold and seal it, and direct it to the *Times*.

"Now put it in thy pocket, and promise it shall go into post as you go home."

"But, Mr. Wishart," said I, in great perplexity, "surely you will let me tell your daughter? it is not right to take such a step without her knowledge."

"Give me the letter," snapped he, savagely, "I see I can't trust 'ee. I'll find a way to send it. Oh! Lord—Lord! to think I should live to be such a helpless creter, as can't walk a quarter of a mile, if t'were to save my own life!" then, in a coaxing voice, he added, "I didn't think ye had been so hard-hearted to an old man; put it in thy pocket—here's Hannah coming, don't let her see it."

Frightened by the agitation he displayed, I hurriedly did as he implored me, and had just concealed the letter when his daughter entered with the pens he had sent her for.

Master Wishart's eyes twinkled with malicious pleasure as she placed them on the table, and he said, "Thank'ee lass—thank'ee, but I don't want 'em now; young madam has wrote what I wanted with the old one."

Mrs. Locksley looked at me with some surprise, as I stood confused, and uncertain how to act. Ought I to send the letter without her sanction? The farmer keenly scanned my face while I stood irresolute, then addressing his daughter, he said,

"You have been gone a long time, Hannah, I s'pose you have been gossiping with Mother Standen. The young madam wants to be off. Say good-bye to her here, I can't spare 'ee to go to the door with her. Come and help me up, and I'll try and get as far as the egg cupboard—it's many a day since I've handled 'em."

Thus summarily dismissed, I had no resource but to quit the house with the letter and money in my possession.

During my walk home, I revolved in my mind all the circumstances connected with my late visit. The old man was capable of acting on his own judgment, and it was no unreasonable desire to wish for his grandchild's presence; and yet I felt an insuperable aversion to being the means through which she might return to Brookfields. Her poor mother, it was evident, did not wish her to do so, and, knowing this, would it be right to humour her father at her expense?

In this state of uncertainty I reached the

turning which led to the Vicarage, and resolved to take my doubts and perplexities to my friends there.

No one was at home but the elder Mrs. Hurst when I arrived there, but she consented to take charge of the letter, and tell her son all that related to it."

"You may safely trust to him to act for the best, my dear," said the venerable lady. "If he does not think it right to forward it without Mrs. Locksley's knowledge, he will return it to the farmer, and endeavour to persuade him to consult with his daughter respecting the prudence of inserting such an advertisement. Philip shall write to you at Baymouth, and tell you the results of his interference."

END OF VOL. I.

F. Shoberl, Printer, 37, Dean Street, Soho, W.

www.ingramcontent.com/pod-product-compliance
Lightning Source LLC
Chambersburg PA
CBHW021202230426
43667CB00006B/517